LIVE RICHER NOW

100 Simple Ways to Become INSTANTLY Richer

Written by **JACOB SAGER WEINSTEIN**

Illustrated by **LAUREN RADLEY**

odd dot

NEW YORK

For the members of Picturebookies, past and present—
the best group of peer mentors (page 22) an author could have

"The business schools reward difficult complex
behavior more than simple behavior, but
simple behavior is more effective."
—Warren Buffett

An imprint of Macmillan Children's Publishing Group, LLC
120 Broadway, New York, NY 10271 • OddDot.com
Odd Dot ® is a registered trademark of Macmillan Publishing Group, LLC

Joyful Books for Curious Minds

The Be Better Now Series is a trademark of Odd Dot.

WRITER Jacob Sager Weinstein
ILLUSTRATOR Lauren Radley
DESIGNERS Tim Hall and Caitlyn Hunter
EDITOR Justin Krasner
VETTER Rachel Sanborn Lawrence, CFP®, MSFP

Library of Congress Cataloging-in-Publication Data is available.

ISBN 978-1-250-79509-0

Our books are available at special discounts when purchased in bulk for premiums and
sales promotions as well as for fund-raising or educational use. Special editions or book
excerpts also can be created to specification. For details, contact the Macmillan Corporate
and Premium Sales Department at (800) 221-7945 ext. 5442, or send an email to
MacmillanSpecialMarkcts@macmillan.com.

First edition, 2024
Printed in China by Hung Hing Printing

10 9 8 7 6 5 4 3 2 1

CONTENTS

RICHER SPENDING 97

INTRODUCTION

I want to acknowledge a truth that is rarely uttered in books on personal finance: Our economy is not fair.

Some people earn their prosperity through hard work and smart choices. Others are just as smart and hardworking but don't get far because of systemic injustice or plain bad luck.

As a result, I'm always skeptical of finance writers who refuse to acknowledge their own good fortune. Let me acknowledge mine right now: My mom was an immigrant, and my father was the grandson of immigrants. Thanks to my parents' lifetime of hard work, and through no virtue of my own, I was born into a level of financial comfort far above what they were born into. Like the majority of homeowners (page 68), my wife and I had help from loved ones when we bought our first home. Perhaps most valuably, my parents taught me everything they had learned about the value of investments, the risks of credit, and the building blocks of success.

In writing *Live Richer Now*, I've also sought out the best financial advice I could find from some of the smartest people around, and I've presented it as simple, achievable things you can do right now.

Some tips may surprise you. Did you know that working fewer hours is often the secret to getting more done? (page 28). Even when I'm offering advice you've probably heard before, I've tried to drill into the specifics you may not know. How much of a savings cushion do you need? See page 60. How can you network effectively? See pages 36–40.

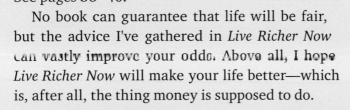

No book can guarantee that life will be fair, but the advice I've gathered in *Live Richer Now* can vastly improve your odds. Above all, I hope *Live Richer Now* will make your life better—which is, after all, the thing money is supposed to do.

ICONS TO LOOK FOR:

You'll notice a few recurring logos. Here's what they mean.

RULE OF THUMB

Throughout this book, I'll offer rules of thumb—rough guides that let you make good choices without a PhD in mathematics. You can spot them by looking for this icon.

LEARN MORE

Every page in *Live Richer Now* boils complex financial ideas into simple, actionable advice. But some topics merit deeper dives. This icon will point you to books and websites with additional information.

RICH
BEGINNINGS

Let's start with some important financial principles, from setting your goals to calculating your net worth. This section will give you the most basic building blocks of financial success.

BE REALISTIC ABOUT HOW HAPPY MONEY WILL MAKE YOU

Earning enough to feed your family will make you happier. Earning enough to buy a third private jet won't. But what about in between? At what point does income become untethered from happiness?

Before I answer that, I need to define some terms.

Affect is how you feel in the moment. **Life evaluation** is your view of your overall well-being.

To understand the difference, imagine you're at the funeral of a beloved elderly aunt. You'd be sad that she died, so you'd have a negative affect. But surrounded by your large and loving family, you might have a positive life evaluation.

For single people in the US, life evaluation peaks at an income of around $105,000. That's right: Single Americans who earn $160,000 per year are, on average, *less* satisfied with their lives than those who earn $105,000. It's not a big drop, but it's noticeable in the data.

Similarly, positive affect peaks at $65,000. Again, that's a *peak*—a single American who earns $130,000 a year is less likely to feel happy at a given moment than somebody who is earning half that.

The relationship between money and happiness is a **correlation**. A correlation means two things tend to go together, but it doesn't tell you which causes the other. Maybe having too much money makes you unhappy. Or maybe unhappy people distract themselves by doing more work, which earns them more cash.

Note that the numbers in question are averages across the entire country. Depending on your local cost of living, you might need to adjust them upward or downward.

STEP 1: If you're single with an income below $65,000 (or married with a combined income below $130,000) and you expect that more money will make you happier, you're probably right. Carry on with this book.

STEP 2: If you're single with an income between $65,000 and $105,000 (or married with a joint income from $130,000 to $210,000), extra money is unlikely to give you more happy moments, but it may increase your overall life satisfaction. Ask yourself where that life satisfaction will come from. Will it be something healthy, like increased stability? Or unhealthy, like status symbols that don't bring you joy?

STEP 3: If you're single with an income above $105,000 (or married with a joint income above $210,000), ask yourself if you'd be better off making less money and having more time to spend on the things that bring you joy.

☐ If you've considered your personal relationship between money and happiness, consider it a win.

APPRECIATE WHAT YOU ALREADY HAVE

Besides *Live Richer Now*, I wrote *Be Happier Now, Live Smarter Now,* and *Be Healthier Now*. You can probably tell I'm a big believer in self-improvement.

But there's a little-discussed problem with self-improvement: The more goals you set, the less time you feel you have. And feeling time-rich has been shown to make you happier than feeling money-rich. Fortunately, there's a solution. The evidence suggests that focusing on what you already have can help restore your sense of having time to spare.

STEP 1: Make a list of ways in which you're already rich. Do you go to bed on a full stomach? Have you vacationed somewhere beautiful? Are you able to spend time with people you love?

STEP 2: Compare your life to medieval royalty. Is your home heated better than a drafty stone castle? Do you own a magical device that summons music by the greatest performers of the age? Can you put cinnamon on your food any time you want, without sending caravans of merchants on epic treks? If so, you aren't living like a king; you are living better.

STEP 3: Read the rest of this book for advice on making more money—but don't lose sight of what you've already got.

☐ If you've identified ways in which you're already rich, you're already a winner.

KNOW WHAT YOU'RE WORKING FOR

Money should be a tool, not an end in itself. Before we start talking about how to get richer, think about *why* you want to get richer. Do you want to own your own home? Pay for your children's college education? Purchase the entire print run of *Live Richer Now*? (Hey, I've got my own financial goals to work toward.)

STEP 1: Ask yourself, "What are my long-term goals in life?"

STEP 2: Think about your core values. If you had to rank things like prestige, family, making the world better, and having fun, what order would you put them in? What else would you put on the list?

STEP 3: Make sure your goals align with your values. If they don't, rethink them.

STEP 4: Once you're happy that your goals are aligned with your values, ask yourself, "Which of those goals requires money? How much money will I need for them? When will I need it?"

STEP 5: People's goals and values evolve over time. Check in with yourself often to make sure you're not chasing something you no longer find meaningful.

☐ If you've defined what you're working for, you've worked up a win.

BREAK BIG GOALS INTO SMALL ONES

It's good to have ambitious financial goals—but it can be overwhelming. Breaking down huge, long-term goals into concrete things you can do today makes them much more achievable. In fact, that's the philosophy of the entire Be Better Now series.

STEP 1: Consider a big financial or career goal you want to accomplish this year.

STEP 2: Figure out what you have to do every week to accomplish that goal a year from now. Breaking down some goals is a matter of simple math—a $6,000 IRA contribution is $115.38 a week. Others may require some careful strategic planning. If you want a new job, how much time should you devote to updating your resume, how much to improving your skills, etc.?

STEP 3: Break those weekly goals down even further. What do you need to do today to be where you want to be a week from now? To reach that $6,000 IRA deposit, can you shave $16.48 from your daily expenses?

☐ If you've taken one small step toward a big goal, give yourself a big win.

DEFINE SUCCESS TO ACHIEVE SUCCESS

It's not enough to think about goals; you need to document them, too. Thanks to a psychological phenomenon called **hindsight bias**, our present-day opinions can change our memories of what we used to believe, and even what we did. A few months after the Super Bowl, a certain number of people who bet on the losing team will genuinely believe they bet on the winners.

Having a written record of your original intentions can help keep you honest.

STEP 1: For any specific task you're undertaking in the near future, ask yourself: What will success look like? Will it be a subjective goal ("I'll make my next batch of brownies even tastier than the last") or an objective one ("I'll increase sales at my bakery by 5 percent in the next three months")? Will your measurement be based on input ("I'll spend 100 hours trying new recipes") or output ("I will bake fifty varieties of brownie")?

STEP 2: Write down your goals.

STEP 3: When the task is over, measure it against your stated goals. Where did you succeed? Where did you fail?

STEP 4: Reflect on your goals. If you succeeded, was it because your goals stretched and challenged you—or because they were too easy? If you failed, was it because you didn't live up to your goals—or because you set impossible standards for yourself?

> ☐ If you've defined success for one goal, large or small, you've met my definition of success.

FRAME BROADLY

Attention to detail is usually a good thing. If somebody is performing heart surgery on me, I want her exquisitely attuned to every fluctuation in my vital signs.

In investing, though, there's such a thing as too much attention to detail. Studies show that people who check their investments every day may do worse than those who check them less frequently.

That's because a key aspect of investing is **broad framing**—focusing on the overall context, rather than the minute details. Imagine a stock price that drops 3 cents this week, drops 10 cents next week, goes up 50 cents the week after, and drops 10 cents the week after that. If you're tracking it closely, you'll notice losses three out of four weeks. You might be tempted to sell. You'll certainly get stressed. But somebody who checks the price once a month will see that it's gone up 27 cents. That's a more useful and less nerve-racking perspective.

Note that this entry applies to long-term investments, which you can expect to go up and down. If you've got money in a savings account, ticking away at a steady interest rate, you probably won't be tempted to check it every day—but there's no harm if you do.

STEP 1: Practice broad framing when making new investments. Don't just ask yourself, "How risky is this one investment?" Ask, "Do I want more or less risk in my overall portfolio? Does this investment move me closer toward that goal?"

. . . .

STEP 2: Practice broad framing when judging the investments you already have. Don't think, "I'm an idiot for losing money on this one stock." Do think, "Including winners and losers, my overall portfolio is up 10 percent."

STEP 3: Practice broad framing across time. Don't even look at how your long-term investments are doing on most days. Once every few months is plenty. Even then, stay focused on long-term performance, rather than month-to-month fluctuations.

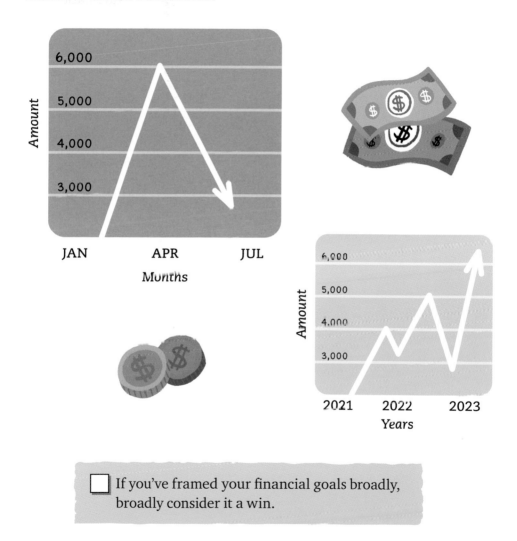

If you've framed your financial goals broadly, broadly consider it a win.

NO.

As Warren Buffett once said, "The difference between successful people and very successful people is that very successful people say no to almost everything."

Life is short. There's not enough time to accomplish everything you want to accomplish. There's *definitely* not enough time to accomplish everything other people want you to accomplish.

STEP 1: If somebody asks you to do something, ask yourself, "Am I excited to do this? Is it meaningful or fun, like a trip to an amusement park with my nieces?"

. . . .

STEP 2: If not, ask yourself, "Am I morally obligated to do this? Will ten innocent people and a puppy die if I say no?"

. . . .

STEP 3: If not, ask yourself, "Is this one of the most advantageous things I can do with the finite hours I have left in my life?"

. . . .

STEP 4: If you haven't gotten to a "hell yes!" with any of the previous questions, the answer is "hell no!" (Or at least, that's the answer in your head. Out loud, you can always say, "No, thank you" or "I'm afraid that's not possible.")

☐ If you've said no to one thing, say yes to a win.

ADD UP YOUR HOURS

Time is money—but just how much?

STEP 1: If you're paid by the hour, write down how much money you take home per hour, after taxes. Otherwise, take your annual after-tax salary, divide it by the rough number of hours you work per day, and write that down.

STEP 2: Imagine you were planning to spend an hour doing something you find enjoyable or meaningful. Somebody calls you up and asks you to spend that hour working instead. How much would they have to pay you to say yes? Write down that number, too.

STEP 3: Now imagine you're about to do an hour's worth of some chore that you feel neutral about—something you don't particularly mind but don't particularly enjoy. What's the maximum amount you'd pay somebody to do it for you?

STEP 4: Average all three numbers. This will give you a very rough dollar value for one hour of your time.

STEP 5: Keep that value in mind any time you trade time for money, or vice versa. If you spend an hour bargain-hunting to save $10, and your time is worth $80 per hour, you've just lost $70.

STEP 6: When in doubt, give up money to gain minutes, rather than vice versa; studies show that extra time makes you happier than extra cash. See page 117 for more on this.

☐ If you've calculated a rough value for your time, spend a few cents acknowledging the win.

CALCULATE YOUR NET WORTH

If you want to improve your financial situation, a simple net worth calculation will give you an idea of where you are and where you need to go.

STEP 1: Make a list of your **assets** from the cash in your wallet to the contents of your retirement account. In theory, your assets include every object you own. In practice, it's not worth listing stuff you couldn't realistically sell for a significant chunk of change. Start with the most valuable items and work your way down until it feels silly; for most people, the threshold value is between $200 and $500.

STEP 2: Include the cash value of every asset on your list. For physical stuff you could sell, list the money you would realistically get for it. If your laptop is going for $500 on eBay, it doesn't matter that you paid $3,000 for it many years ago. Its current cash value is $500.

STEP 3: Make a list of your **liabilities**—the money you owe. This includes credit card debt, mortgages, student loans, medical debt, money borrowed from family and friends, and anything in collections.

STEP 4: Add up your assets, then subtract your liabilities. The result is your net worth. Don't stress if it's a negative number! Your current net worth is your starting point, not your destiny.

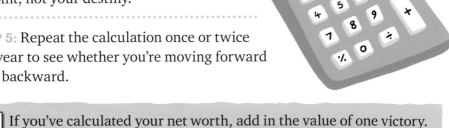

STEP 5: Repeat the calculation once or twice a year to see whether you're moving forward or backward.

☐ If you've calculated your net worth, add in the value of one victory.

PRIORITIZE YOUR TASKS BY PROFIT

On any given day, you *could* do an infinite number of things to improve your financial situation. But unless you've found a savings account that pays interest in minutes, you only have twenty-four hours to do them. It's tempting to start with the things that came up most recently or that somebody else is nagging you to do. But there's a better way to prioritize.

STEP 1: Make a list of all the money-related tasks you could do right now—little ones like getting a refund on that moldy fruit, and big ones like setting up an IRA and putting $1,000 in it.

STEP 2: Estimate how many hours each task would take you. (Returning fruit: half an hour. Setting up an IRA: one hour.)

STEP 3: Estimate how much money you would save or earn by completing each task. (Returning fruit: $4.50. Setting up your IRA, even if you never put in more than this one deposit: $64,000 by the time you retire in a few decades.)

STEP 4: Divide the money by the hours. That's the rough profit-per-hour of each task. (Fruit: $9 per hour. IRA: $64,000 per hour.)

STEP 5: Do the task that earns you the most per hour. Set up your retirement account, and swallow the loss on the fruit. (Don't swallow the fruit, though, or you might not make it to retirement.) If that task seems overwhelming, you can break it into more manageable steps (page 6).

> ☐ If you've prioritized your tasks by profit-per-hour, give yourself the win.

LEARN TO USE A SPREADSHEET

When the computer spreadsheet was invented in 1979, it transformed personal computing—and personal finance. If you aren't using one, you're missing out on one of the most powerful financial tools of the modern world. The good news is: It's not hard to learn the basics.

STEP 1: Find a spreadsheet program. You don't have to shell out a lot of money. Numbers is free for Mac users, and Open Office is free for most operating systems. Google Sheets is free for anybody with a web browser.

STEP 2: Play around with it. Put a number in box A1. Put a number in box A2. Then in box A3, type "=A1+A2". Notice what happens when you change the numbers in the first two boxes. (FYI: In spreadsheet-speak, each box is called a "cell.")

STEP 3: Try more complex equations. And instead of typing "A1" or "A2," just click on the appropriate cell to insert its number into an equation.

STEP 4: Search a video site for "spreadsheet basics" to learn more.

STEP 5: Next time you're buying a car, budgeting a vacation, or making any other numerical decision, whip out a spreadsheet to compare the options.

1	Which car should I buy?							
2								
3	Model	Initial cost	How many years will it last?	MPG	Cost of gas per gallon	Miles driven per year	Annual gas cost	Annual cost of car
4	Cheapo 4000	$2,000.00	3	5	$4.00	1000	$800.00	$1,466.67
5	Value XLNT	$5,000.00	5	30	$4.00	1000	$133.33	$1,133.33
6								

□ If you've learned spreadsheet basics, or used a spreadsheet to help make a decision, enter "I won!" into any cell you want.

BE FOXY

In 1953, Isaiah Berlin published an essay called *The Hedgehog and the Fox*, inspired by a quote from Greek poet Archilochus: "The fox knows many things, but the hedgehog knows one big thing." Berlin divided human thinkers between hedgehogs like Nietzsche (whose writing centered on one big idea) and foxes like Shakespeare (who plucked details from all aspects of human experience).

A rich literary diet might include both foxes and hedgehogs. But as author Jim Collins found when he studied top-performing companies, multifaceted foxes make better corporate leaders. Other studies found foxes are better at predicting future trends (page 17).

If you're writing a philosophical manifesto, feel free to hedgehog away. But when you're planning your financial future, think like a fox.

STEP 1: When making a financial decision, resist a single grand theory about what will be profitable. Take in as many pieces of evidence as possible, and view them through multiple viewpoints.

. . . .

STEP 2: Don't let the fox-and-hedgehog theory become your single grand theory, either! View it as a useful guide, rather than a hard-and-fast rule.

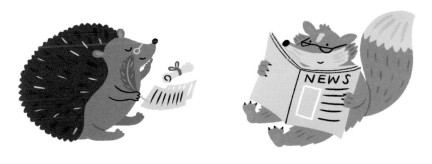

☐ If you've resisted the urge to see the world through a single lens, take many small wins.

FIGHT DECISION FATIGUE

If you carefully negotiate every penny on the purchase of your new car, then give in at the end and buy a ridiculously expensive undercoating option, you may be suffering from **decision fatigue**. Psychologists might use the more technical term **ego depletion**. Whatever you call it, your brain needs a certain amount of energy to maintain discipline and focus. When it's gone, you're more likely to make lazy decisions.

In our twenty-four-hour, online, connected world, you might not be able to completely avoid decision fatigue. But a few techniques can help you stave it off.

I won't eat out more than once a week.

STEP 1: If you know you'll have to make a bunch of decisions in a row, make the most consequential ones first, while you're still fresh. Figure out your wedding budget before you start thinking about the font size for the invites.

STEP 2: Whenever possible, break up bouts of decision-making. At the very least, take a few minutes to walk around the room or eat a piece of fruit to keep your blood sugar up.

STEP 3: Come up with rules of thumb for daily life so you don't have to expend energy repeatedly on the same decisions. (I've suggested several of them throughout this book—look for the Rule of Thumb logo.)

Every year on my birthday, I'll put money in my IRA.

STEP 4: Set up auto deposit into your retirement and savings accounts, allowing you to make an investment decision once and stick with it.

☐ If you've taken steps to stave off decision fatigue, decide to count it as a win.

SEE THE FUTURE

Financial planning is all about predictions. Will a certain stock go up or down? If you take out an auto loan, will you regret it three years from now?

Wharton professor Philip Tetlock has discovered certain principles used by **superforecasters**—people with an uncanny knack for seeing what will come next.

To learn more, read *Superforecasting: The Art and Science of Prediction* by Philip Tetlock.

STEP 1: There are no certainties, so frame your predictions in terms of probabilities. "There's an 80 percent chance that Apple stock will rise" is a more nuanced forecast than "Apple stock will rise."

STEP 2: The way you ask a question can bias your answer, so ask yourself multiple versions. Ask yourself, "What are the odds that Apple will go up?" *and* "What are the odds that Apple will go down or stay the same?" If your answers don't add to 100 percent, there's a flaw in your logic.

STEP 3: Perform a **premortem**. Imagine it's the future and your prediction turned out to be wrong. Ask yourself: What went wrong? ("A new, inexpensive Android model ate heavily into Apple's market share.")

STEP 4: Now come back to the present. How can you factor this possible failure into your prediction?

STEP 5: Put your prediction aside for two weeks. Then, without looking at your old prediction, think through the issue and make a new prediction. Compare it with your old one. Which one is now more convincing?

STEP 6: Seek out thoughtful people to discuss your predictions. Tetlock found teams of superforecasters to be 24 percent more accurate than individuals.

☐ If you've thought like a superforecaster, I predict a victory.

TALK TO A PROFESSIONAL

I've tried to provide advice that will apply to as many people as possible. But no two people have the same financial situation, and no book can cover every possibility. For expert advice tailored to your personal situation, speak to a professional.

STEP 1: Find a reputable financial advisor. If you have friends whose judgment you trust, ask them for recommendations. You can also ask trusted professionals in other fields—your CPA might know somebody, for example.

STEP 2: No matter who recommended the advisor, do your own homework. Type their name into **brokercheck.finra.org** (and maybe a search engine or two) and see if any red flags turn up. Ask for references.

STEP 3: Also check their credentials. If you need something beyond budget and debt coaching, consider a Certified Financial Planner (CFP). CFPs have to have extensive experience, and they're required to act in the best interests of their clients.

STEP 4: Make sure you understand how a potential advisor makes their money (page 62). If they get a commission on everything they sell you, they have an incentive to sell you stuff whether you need it or not. If they get a percentage of the money they manage, they an incentive to steer you away from accounts they don't manage, like your employee pension plan, even if those are the best options for you. That doesn't mean you should reject their advice out of hand; it does mean you'll need keep an eye out for conflicts of interest.

STEP 5: See below for examples of potential questions you might ask the advisor to help you with. If you don't have specific questions, it's fair to tell them about your values and investment goals (page 5) and ask what they'd recommend.

Things You Can Ask an Advisor About

- Should I have a Health Savings Account (HSA) and/or a Flexible Savings Account (FSA)?

- What kind of retirement plan should I be investing in—a Roth IRA, a traditional IRA, an employer retirement plan, or something else?

- What approach should I take to paying my debts down?

- How much of an emergency fund should I set up?

- Given my specific financial situation and goals, what should my top priority be?

☐ If you've spoken to a Certified Financial Planner (or even just set up an appointment with one), I advise you to consider it a victory.

READ THE FINE PRINT

My dad is a lawyer. Among the bits of legal wisdom he passed on to me: A lawyer who represents himself has a fool for a client, never sign a contract you haven't read, and always read the fine print.

People who don't heed the last two can find themselves locked into long-term contracts for products they don't need or deprived of the right to sue if something goes wrong.

STEP 1: If you're signing a contract, read it before you sign. If there's anything you don't want to be legally bound by, don't sign it.

STEP 2: If you're purchasing a good or service that comes with a lot of fine print, read the fine print before you buy to make sure you're getting what you think you're getting.

STEP 3: I know it's not always realistic to read the encyclopedic fine print on every app or website—but if you make a conscious choice to skip it, recognize that you're entering unknown territory.

☐ If you've read the fine print, then you agree to all relevant terms and conditions of *Live Richer Now,* in all media past and future, throughout the universe, wherever you take a win.

RICHER YOU

Your stocks can crash. Your house can burn down. But the time and money you invest in yourself will always pay off in the long run. That's why *you* are your biggest and most important investment.

GET A MENTOR

Studies show that people with mentors have faster promotions, higher salaries, and greater career satisfaction. But how do you get one? And once you have one, how do you get the most out of the relationship?

These tips come from the work of management professors Wendy Murphy and Kathy E. Kram.

To learn more, read *Strategic Relationships at Work: Creating Your Circle of Mentors, Sponsors, and Peers for Success in Business and Life* by Wendy Murphy and Kathy E. Kram.

STEP 1: If you're working on a project with (or for) somebody senior, start the ball rolling by asking for their feedback. Alternatively, you can ask a potential mentor for an informational interview. Come prepared with thoughtful questions about their career path.

STEP 2: Did your potential mentor seem welcoming of your questions? Did you both enjoy the conversation? If so, reach out to them again. If future meetings go well, you can explicitly ask them to be your mentor, or you can just keep the relationship going without labeling it.

STEP 3: Don't look at yourself as the passive recipient of your mentor's wisdom. You can influence how much mentoring you receive by being eager, prepared, and grateful.

STEP 4: Look for these developmental relationships within your workplace, but don't look *exclusively* within your workplace. An outside mentor can offer a fresh perspective and help you look for opportunities beyond your current employer.

STEP 5: If your workplace has a formal mentoring program, take advantage of it. But keep pursuing informal mentoring relationships, which tend to be more effective than formal ones.

STEP 6: You will change over time, and so will your professional needs. If there comes a time when the guidance you're getting from your mentor is no longer helpful, you're allowed to move on. Depending on how formal your relationship is, you can explicitly (but politely and gratefully) end things or just gradually stop seeking out their advice.

STEP 7: Go beyond a single mentor. Pursue a **developmental network**—multiple people who can help you with different aspects of your career and personal growth. This might include a **reverse mentor** (somebody younger or in a junior position who nonetheless has things to teach you); a **mentoring circle** (where two or three mentors help a group of mentees); a **sponsor** (who helps advance your career but doesn't offer emotional support); a **coach** (who offers focused help on specific skills); and **peer mentors** (who are at or very near your level).

☐ If you've worked with a mentor or taken one step toward finding one, give yourself the win.

GET A MENTEE

In a mentor/mentee relationship, it's not just the mentee who benefits. Studies show that being a mentor is associated with higher career satisfaction and more success.

As always with associations, a caveat is in order: It's hard to know which is the cause and which is the effect. Maybe mentoring makes you more satisfied and successful; maybe being more satisfied and successful makes you want to mentor. Either way, the evidence seems clear: Being a mentor is often part of a happy career.

STEP 1: If somebody younger or less experienced asks for your advice, take the time to speak with them. Don't just lecture them; get a sense of what they are looking for out of the meeting.

STEP 2: You don't have to wait to be asked. Reach out to people you know who might need guidance, or put out feelers within your network to let people know you are available.

STEP 3: If certain groups are underrepresented in your field, they may be underrepresented in your pool of potential mentees. Make extra effort to ensure your mentee selection doesn't perpetuate a systemic bias.

STEP 4: If an initial meeting goes well, stay in touch. A younger or less experienced person might not want to bother you; let them know if you're open to future conversations.

STEP 5: You can formally offer to be their mentor, or you can just informally keep channels of communication open. Mentoring isn't the only way you can help somebody develop—there are many roles in a developmental network (page 22).

STEP 6: Be open to "reverse mentoring"—to learning from your mentee. If they are lower down in your organization, they may know more than you about how things work on the front lines. If they are younger than you, they may be more in touch with modern technology and trends.

STEP 7: A mentorship doesn't have to be forever. You can explicitly set a time frame or just let things fade if you feel the relationship has run its course.

☐ If you've helped a mentee, help yourself to a win.

EXTINGUISH BURNOUT

In 2019, the World Health Organization (WHO) officially recognized burnout as "a syndrome . . . resulting from chronic workplace stress that has not been successfully managed." If you're suffering from it, you're not alone. In some professions, it runs rampant; surveys found signs of burnout in 30 percent of teachers and a whopping 68.6 percent of oncologists.

Signs of Burnout

According to the WHO's official definition, burnout is characterized by:

- Feelings of energy depletion or exhaustion.
- Increased mental distance from one's job, or feelings of cynicism related to one's job.
- Reduced professional efficacy.

STEP 1: If you're suffering from the signs of burnout, evaluate your job in terms of six key areas: **workload**, **control**, **reward**, **community**, **fairness**, and **values**.

STEP 2: If your **workload** is excessive, look for opportunities to reduce it or at least take a break from it. Can you delegate more? Use some of your vacation days, paid or unpaid?

STEP 3: If you don't have enough **control** over your work, look for opportunities to gain some. Can you get more involved in decision-making? Or ask your boss to give you the authority you need to accomplish what you're expected to do?

STEP 4: If you're not getting **rewarded** for your work, look for opportunities to get more recognition, financial or otherwise. Can you ask for a raise? Or nominate yourself for a workplace award?

STEP 5: If your workplace **community** is lacking, look for opportunities to strengthen it. Can you get away from your desk and spend lunchtime with a coworker? Or schedule a meeting with a colleague to solve a problem that both of you face?

STEP 6: If your workplace lacks **fairness**, look for opportunities to make things more fair. Can you join with other employees to point out the problems to management? Or change processes to be more equitable?

STEP 7: If your job and your **values** are out of step, look for opportunities to bring them more in sync. Can you focus on work tasks that are more personally meaningful? Or direct your organization's energy toward a worthwhile end?

STEP 8: If you answered any of the above questions with, "Don't ask me! Ask my freaking boss!!!", that's an entirely reasonable response. Burnout is frequently the fault of the workplace, not the workers. If you're not getting the support you need, it may be time to look for a new job. And in the meantime, treat yourself with as much kindness and compassion as you can, and consider getting therapy if it's available to you.

☐ If you've recognized the signs of burnout or taken steps to prevent it, give yourself the win.

WORK LESS TO DO MORE

In 2019, Microsoft's Japanese division tried a crazy experiment: They paid their workers for a five-day workweek but made them work only four. To discourage employees from sneaking in extra labor, Microsoft subsidized any family trips, classes, or volunteer work they did on their bonus day off.

And how much productivity did Microsoft lose by chopping off one-fifth of their workweek?

None. In fact, productivity went *up* 40 percent.

Microsoft's experiment was the latest demonstration of something labor experts have known for a century: In many circumstances, fewer hours mean more work done. An extra day of rest can pay dividends over the entire week that follows. People who work forty to fifty hours a week consistently accomplish more in the long run than people who work sixty hours. Sometimes, people who work thirty-five hours get even *more* done.

STEP 1: If your job is based on output, rather than number of hours in the office, try spending fewer hours doing your work. If your job monitors the number of hours you work, see if your boss will let you work fewer hours if you can get the same amount done. If you manage a team, try letting everybody work fewer hours.

STEP 2: See if the extra rest and relaxation boosts your productivity.

STEP 3: If you don't have the privilege of setting your own hours, and you can't find a job that lets you work fewer than fifty hours a week, be kind to yourself. If you're inefficient under those circumstances, it's not your fault.

STEP 4: If you have a short-term deadline, you may be able to pull off sixty-hour workweeks for up to two months without a net loss in productivity. But don't try to keep it going for longer than that, and make sure you schedule vacation time afterward.

☐ If you've improved your productivity by working fewer hours, take the time to acknowledge your win.

NETWORK EFFECTIVELY

Networking is a crucial career tool. Studies have found that better networkers have higher career satisfaction, larger salaries, and better performance reviews.

It comes naturally for some lucky souls. For the rest of us, a few tips are in order.

STEP 1: **Preintroduce yourself.** If somebody you want to meet will be at an upcoming event, drop them a quick email to say you hope to see them there. If a mutual friend can make the introduction, even better.

STEP 2: Networking consists of three parts: making new contacts, staying in touch with the contacts you have, and using your contacts. The staying in touch part is crucial; one deep connection rooted in shared experience is more useful (and more personally meaningful) than collecting a dozen business cards.

STEP 3: Don't be so focused on **external networking** (contacts with people outside your workplace) that you neglect **internal networking** (contacts with people at your place of work). One study found that staying in touch with contacts in your workplace was correlated more strongly with salary growth and career satisfaction than any aspect of external networking.

STEP 4: By all means, attend networking events within your field, but don't miss out on the rest of life. Volunteer on charity boards. Take classes in new fields. Your main reward will be a richer, fuller life—but a side benefit is that you'll expand your network in new and unpredictable ways. Shared activities are a potent way of cementing relationships.

STEP 5: Whether there's a massive global pandemic or a localized outbreak of food poisoning, sometimes events get canceled. That doesn't have to stop you from connecting. Drop a note to a fellow would-be attendee to say you had looked forward to meeting up with them. Ask if you can set a time to video chat.

☐ If you've done one aspect of networking right, make a connection with a big win.

NETWORK HORIZONTALLY

It's 1963. You're a page at NBC studios in New York. You ignore your fellow peons and focus on the bigwigs. Finally, you end up in an elevator with Johnny Carson. You pitch him a joke. He laughs but doesn't hire you. Well, that's okay—you did absolutely everything you could to network.

Or did you? Remember those other pages you ignored? One of them was Michael Eisner, who went on to spend two decades as CEO of Disney.

You were so busy **vertical networking** (making contacts with people above you) that you neglected **horizontal networking** (making contacts with people at your own level). You and Michael could have spent your careers lifting each other. With Michael's help, you could have ended up hosting your own talk show. With your help, Michael could have spent *three* decades as CEO.

Even if you're not in show business, horizontal networking can be a crucial path to success in your field.

STEP 1: Look for opportunities to get to know people at roughly your level.

STEP 2: Be alert to the ways you and your horizontal contacts can help one another— but be even more alert to the ways you enjoy one another's company. Networking rooted in genuine friendship is more likely to last—and it's much more fun.

STEP 3: See page 30 for tips on effective networking; they apply just as much to horizontal networks as vertical.

> ☐ If you've made a contact at your own level or reached out to a contact you already have, you've connected with victory.

MNETWORK MNEMONICALLY

Remembering the people you've already met is a crucial part of networking, but it never came naturally to me.

When I began researching memory techniques, I learned that absent-mindedness is not a life sentence. There are techniques you can use to help names and faces stick.

To learn more, read *How to Remember Everything: Tips & Tricks to Become a Memory Master* by Jacob Sager Weinstein.

STEP 1: Before somebody introduces themselves, silently guess what their name is. You're unlikely to be right—but correcting a wrong guess will help make their real name stick.

STEP 2: Find a distinctive visual image that sounds like their name, and imagine it somewhere on their face. Picture olives replacing Olivia's eyes or Mohammed wearing a mohawk.

STEP 3: As he was speaking with people, Bill Clinton used to write down their details on an index card. I don't have Bill Clinton's chutzpah, so I jot down a few details about the person and our conversation later, in private.

STEP 4: I quiz myself on my notes using **spaced repetition**, aka reviewing flash cards at steadily increasing intervals. Search the app store of your choice for "spaced repetition" to find a program that will help you do this. Besides my notes, I include a photo of the person if it's available.

☐ If you've used one or more techniques to help you remember names and faces, remember this as a win.

NETWORK HAPPILY

For many of us, networking can feel awkward or even morally wrong.

At least in part, that's because our belief that relationships should be selfless and unforced comes into conflict with the self-interested, deliberate nature of networking.

In theory, you could resolve that conflict by abandoning your belief in true friendship. But it's healthier and more sustainable to find ways to make networking feel less self-interested.

These tips are from business professors Francesca Gino, Maryam Kouchaki, and Tiziana Casciaro, writing in the *Harvard Business Review*.

STEP 1: Instead of framing a work-related social function as a chance to network, think of it as a chance to be exposed to new ideas and perspectives.

STEP 2: When you meet somebody, look for ways your interests and goals align with theirs. Don't just network to help yourself; network to help each other.

STEP 3: Think broadly about what you have to offer the people you're meeting. If they have more expertise or power, you can give them an outside perspective, thoughtful questions, or simply your gratitude for their help.

STEP 4: Put your networking in the context of a higher purpose. Your connections don't just benefit you. They benefit your coworkers and your industry. If you're a member of an underrepresented group, networking increases your visibility, helping smooth the path for others like you.

☐ If you've taken one step to help yourself enjoy networking more, enjoy the win.

LEVEL UP YOUR SKILLS

Acquiring expertise is one of the best investments you can make in yourself. And when it comes to expertise, there was no greater expert than Anders Ericsson. Anders Ericsson found that greatness comes from **deliberate practice**—zooming in on your weak points and getting feedback to improve them.

To learn more, read *Peak: Secrets from the New Science of Expertise* by Anders Ericsson and Robert Pool.

STEP 1: Consider a professional skill you want to improve. For example, do you want to be better at training young Jedi?

STEP 2: Identify your greatest weakness in that area. Do you have a hard time persuading your hotheaded young protégés to stick with their training?

STEP 3: Find an exercise that focuses on that weak point. Recruit the most hotheaded youngling around, and spend hours persuading him to run through mysterious swamps.

STEP 4: If you can, have somebody whose experience you trust observe you and give you constructive feedback. This could be a mentor (page 22), a colleague, or a Force ghost.

STEP 5: Try to be your own source of feedback as well. Whether you do or do not persuade a hothead, review the techniques you tried. Think about how they worked and what differently next time you can do.

STEP 6: When you've strengthened that muscle, identify the next weakness and repeat the process.

☐ If you've used deliberate practice to improve an important career skill, give yourself a deliberate win.

KNOW YOUR BATNA (NEGOTIATING, PART 1)

Negotiating is a crucial life skill, but far too few of us are taught how to do it. These next few entries will cover some important basics. Feel free to jump around the rest of the book, but these tips on negotiation are the rare entries that I recommend you read in order.

Negotiations begin long before you sit down at the table. A crucial first step: figuring out your alternatives.

STEP 1: Imagine that your negotiations fall apart and you can't reach a deal. What would your next-best option be? In business speak, that's your **Best Alternative to Negotiated Agreement**, or **BATNA**. If we're negotiating how much I'll pay you for your old laptop, and your neighbor has already offered you $500 for it, then your BATNA is $500. If you've tried repeatedly and nobody else wants to buy it, your BATNA may be $0.

STEP 2: Also consider BATNAs without an obvious price tag. If nobody buys your laptop, maybe your cousin will teach you how to upgrade it. Instead of cash, you'll gain a new skill. How much money would a buyer have to pay for you to pass up that opportunity?

STEP 3: Figure out whether you can improve your BATNA. Have you checked with your local used-electronics store to see what it would pay? If you install a new operating system, will your neighbor raise his offer?

STEP 4: Consider your opponent's BATNA. If I can't buy your laptop, how much would I have to pay to buy an equivalent one?

STEP 5: Figure out whether you can make your opponent's BATNA worse. If you're just selling a laptop, it's probably not possible. But imagine you're negotiating with your boss for better working conditions. As long as it's just you complaining, his BATNA is "Fire one troublemaker and get a replacement." If you join forces with all your coworkers, his BATNA becomes "Fire everybody and then have to replace an entire workforce."

STEP 6: You know your BATNA, so you know the minimum you'll accept. You know your opponent's BATNA, so you know the maximum they'll offer. As a rule of thumb, you can expect the end result to be somewhere in between.

☐ If you've understood the concept of BATNA or thought about BATNAs before a negotiation, your best alternative is to take the win.

DO YOUR HOMEWORK (NEGOTIATING, PART 2)

Figuring out your BATNA (page 36) is a crucial first step before a negotiation—but it's not the last one. Here are some more steps to take before you sit down at the table. (These tips, and those in the next entries, come from the Harvard Law School's Program on Negotiation.)

STEP 1: There are things you can do during the negotiation to leave on good terms (page 40), but don't wait until then; take relationships into account beforehand, when you're setting your goals.

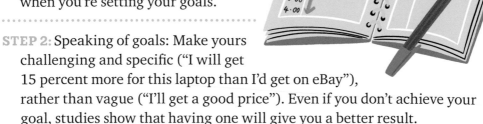

STEP 2: Speaking of goals: Make yours challenging and specific ("I will get 15 percent more for this laptop than I'd get on eBay"), rather than vague ("I'll get a good price"). Even if you don't achieve your goal, studies show that having one will give you a better result.

STEP 3: Identify the questions the other party is likely to ask. Focus on the ones you would least like to hear. ("Why does this laptop smell like it was dropped into a vat of Coca-Cola?") Figure out honest answers that cause the least damage to your position. ("Because it was. But that was a year ago, and it's still working fine.")

STEP 4: Try to come up with concessions that are worth less to you than to the other person. If the deal goes through, you won't have any more use for that laptop case. Why not throw it in for free?

☐ If you've arrived at the negotiating table well prepared, sit down with a win.

THE NEGOTIATION ITSELF
(NEGOTIATING, PART 3)

You've figured out your BATNA. You've done all your other homework. Now it's finally time to sit down at the negotiating table.

STEP 1: If possible, make the initial offer. Thanks to the psychological principle of **anchoring**, the first number we hear tends to define the range we consider reasonable. (Just don't make your offer so far away from their BATNA that negotiations break down before they begin.)

STEP 2: Don't be afraid of silence. If you rush in to fill the gaps in communication, you may end up negotiating against yourself. ("I won't sell this laptop for less than $600 . . . okay, $550 . . . $525?")

STEP 3: Consider revealing your priorities to find areas of mutual benefit. If you're just discussing a single price, this is a moot point. In a multipoint deal, though, you may find that your top priority is something the other party is willing to compromise on. ("You say you want my laptop *and* my kidney. Honestly, I care more about the laptop.") But don't reveal your priorities in your initial offer; wait until you have a better sense of the range of possible outcomes.

STEP 4: Try to meet the goal you set for yourself beforehand, but be realistic. As long as you end up with a deal that beats your BATNA, it was a successful negotiation.

☐ If you've left the table with a good deal, give yourself the win.

LEAVE ON GOOD TERMS (NEGOTIATING, PART 4)

It probably doesn't matter if a car salesman resents you for squeezing his profits on a used Honda, but you don't want to negotiate a salary so intensely that your boss dislikes you on day one.

Fortunately, being a tough negotiator doesn't mean being an unpleasant one. With care, you can walk out of a negotiation with a good deal *and* the other person's respect.

STEP 1: Whenever possible, deliver bad news all at once—but make concessions over multiple steps. That makes the other person feel like they're getting more wins than losses.

STEP 2: Look for opportunities to show respect for the other party's expertise and preferences. ("You want to know how much I'll charge for shipping this laptop? Hmm . . . do you have a shipping service you recommend? I can check on their prices.")

STEP 3: When the other person makes an offer you're happy to accept, don't leap on it. Take some time to think it over. Saying yes too quickly will make them regret not pushing harder.

STEP 4: Once you've reached an agreement, don't express too much happiness or excitement. No matter how good a deal you got, you don't want your opponent to feel taken advantage of.

> ☐ If you and your negotiating partner feel good about your deal, you've both won.

ACT LIKE THE PERSON YOU WANT TO BE

Your personality isn't fixed. By changing what you do, you can actually change who you are.

If you feel your personality is holding you back in your career (or in life), there's a simple technique that has been shown to make lasting changes.

STEP 1: Identify a personality trait you wish you had or wish you had more of. ("I want to be more disciplined.")

STEP 2: Ask yourself: What would you do if you had that trait? Come up with three specific things. ("I'd spend twenty minutes a day studying for my certification exam. I'd stop reading Twitter right before bed. I'd do ten push-ups a day.")

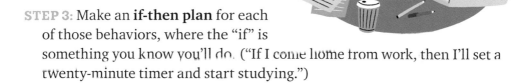

STEP 3: Make an **if-then plan** for each of those behaviors, where the "if" is something you know you'll do. ("If I come home from work, then I'll set a twenty-minute timer and start studying.")

STEP 4: Set a daily reminder on your phone about your if-then plan. For an even bigger motivation boost, ask a friend to check in with you at the end of the day about whether you stuck to it.

STEP 5: Keep going for two weeks.

☐ If you've formulated if-then plans to be the person you want to be (or enacted those plans), then you're the kind of person who deserves the win.

JUMP SHIP

I can't tell you if you should stay at your job or look for a new one. I don't have access to a decade of work and income statistics across the entire country.

But the Federal Reserve Bank of Atlanta does. According to its analysis, people who switch jobs have consistently increased their earnings more than people who didn't.

If your coworkers make every day a joy, or your job is deeply meaningful, you might not care to chase that extra percentage point of annual salary increase. But if there's room for improvement, it may be time to shop around.

STEP 1: If work is making you miserable, or just doesn't leave you with the time or energy to look for a new job, start building up your savings (page 60). Once you have a financial cushion, consider quitting even if you don't have a new job lined up.

STEP 2: If your job is tolerable, stick with it while you hunt for a new one. How intensely you hunt is up to you. Even if you aren't desperate for a new job, keep your ears open for possible opportunities. Having a good external network (page 30) can help with that.

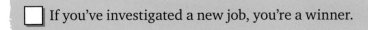

STEP 3: If you get offered a better salary elsewhere, you now have a great BATNA (page 36). You can use it to renegotiate your current salary— or you can just jump ship.

☐ If you've investigated a new job, you're a winner.

PAY YOURSELF FIRST (METAPHORICALLY)

"Pay yourself first": Good advice when applied to budgeting (page 65). Equally good advice when it comes to scheduling.

STEP 1: If something is important to you, make it the first thing you do. Spend thirty minutes improving your professional skills as soon as you wake up, or ten minutes catching up with your boss as soon as you set foot in the office. Don't wait for somebody else to fill up your calendar with their priorities.

my priorities

☐ If you've made your top priority the first thing you do, take the win right away.

BREAK BAD HABITS

No matter how many good financial habits you build, they can be undone by a few bad ones. Fortunately, psychologists have identified the trigger/behavior/reinforcement cycle that cements bad habits. Understanding how it works can help you break them.

STEP 1: Choose a bad habit you want to break.

> To learn more, read *The Power of Habit* by Charles Duhigg.

STEP 2: Pinpoint the **triggers** that prompt the bad **behavior.** If you tend to splurge on purchases you regret, does it happen when you walk past certain stores, or log on to certain websites, or get in certain moods?

STEP 3: Break the routine that includes those triggers. Something as simple as moving your computer to a different room in the house may be enough to stop you from automatically logging on to ExpensiveVinylRecords.com as soon as you boot up.

STEP 4: Identify the **positive reinforcement** the habit gives you. Does dropping $100 on a rare copy of *The Muppet Movie* soundtrack ease the pain of living, or maybe make you feel connected to your idol, Jim Henson?

STEP 5: Find a more constructive way to get that same reinforcement. Ease your cosmic angst by talking with a friend, or feel connected to Jim Henson by watching an old episode of *The Muppet Show*.

☐ If you've worked toward breaking a bad habit, take a win as positive reinforcement.

FIND GOOD INFLUENCES

Thousands of years ago, Aesop wrote, "A man is known by the company he keeps." Science has proved him right: There's considerable evidence that behavior and habits can spread among social groups, for good or for ill.

STEP 1: Think about a behavior that would help you succeed.

STEP 2: Spend time with the friend who embodies that behavior. Trying to cut back on takeout? Hang out with your coworker who always packs their own lunch.

STEP 3: We're not just influenced by what our friends do—we're influenced by what they fail to do. Having a hypocritical friend makes us less likely to believe in the values they claim to hold and more likely to exhibit the vices they really have. Psychologists call this **vicarious dissonance**. If you spend time around a friend who talks a big game but doesn't live up to it, consciously frame it as hypocrisy on their part, rather than an excuse for you to backslide yourself.

If you've spent time with one good influence today, give both of you a win.

MONETIZE YOUR HOBBY

If you enjoy a hobby, and you enjoy making money, why not combine the two?

STEP 1: Consider the things you enjoy doing. Do you like knitting? Or asking rhetorical questions?

....

STEP 2: Think about a way you can monetize it. Can you sell baby booties on Etsy? Or offer debate lessons?

....

STEP 3: Start gradually. Make and advertise a tiny number of booties. Teach a one-time lesson.

....

STEP 4: If you enjoy making cash off your hobby, gradually ramp up. Make more booties! Teach an ongoing seminar in rhetorical techniques!

....

STEP 5: If you find the stresses of running a business are sapping the joy from a pastime you used to love, take a step back. The idea is to make your life better, not worse.

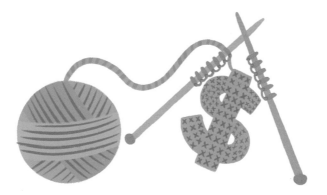

☐ If you've taken a step toward profiting from something you already enjoy doing, give yourself the win.

COLLABORATE WITHOUT GROUPTHINK

Teamwork has always been vital to success, and it's only gotten more so. One study estimated that workers spent 50 percent more time on team activities in 2017 than they did a decade earlier.

At its best, teamwork lets you harness the power of multiple minds. At its worst, teamwork becomes an exercise in **groupthink**—the state where multiple minds reinforce one another's mistakes.

Take the Kennedy White House during the planning of the Bay of Pigs invasion. Together, the brightest minds of America made disastrously poor decisions that resulted in catastrophic failure. To prevent it from happening again, they developed a series of principles to stop groupthink in its tracks. Afterwards, when the Cuban Missile Crisis hit, Kennedy and his cabinet put their heads together far more effectively. They navigated the country safely through a situation where a misstep could have sparked nuclear war.

STEP 1: Meet someplace informal that doesn't belong to any one member of the group. Oval or not, the boss's office is inherently intimidating.

STEP 2: Ask everybody in the group to put aside their personal or departmental interests and act as "skeptical generalists."

STEP 3: If the entire group leans toward a plan, break into subgroups and have each one come up with an alternative. Then reconvene and have each group present their idea.

☐ If you've prevented groupthink, give everybody a win.

SPOT IDENTITY THEFT WHEN IT HAPPENS

Sometimes, despite your best efforts (page 50), you can fall victim to identity theft. Checking your credit report (page 89) is an important step in identifying the problem when it happens. But it's not the only one.

Signs of Identity Theft

The Federal Trade Commission warns that the following are signs of identity theft:

- Seeing unexplained withdrawals from your bank account.

- Not getting your bills or other mail.

- Having checks declined.

- Calls from debt collectors about debts that aren't yours.

- Unfamiliar accounts or charges on your credit report.

- Medical bills for services you didn't use.

- Your health plan unexpectedly rejecting a legitimate claim because its records show you've reached your benefits limit.

- Your medical records showing a condition you don't have.

- An IRS notification that more than one tax return was filed in your name, or that you have income from an unrecognized employer.

- Finding out there was a data breach at a company where you do business or have an account.

STEP 1: Be alert for the signs of identity theft (see sidebar).

STEP 2: If you think your identity has been stolen, go to **IdentityTheft.gov** for tips on how to report it and what steps to take. That's also the website to go to if you lose your credit cards, your driver's license, or any other sensitive personal information.

☐ If you've been alert to the signs of identity theft or handled a theft that occurred, don't let anybody steal your victory.

PROTECT YOUR PRIVACY

Whether or not it's needed for your personal comfort, a bit of privacy is necessary for your financial security. Here are some simple steps you can take to guard against thieves learning more than they should.

STEP 1: The FBI recommends you shred documents with personal or financial information, review your bank and credit card statements each month, and look over your credit report once a year (page 89).

STEP 2: Never give credit card numbers or personal information over the phone, unless you initiated the call to somebody you trust.

STEP 3: If you post on social media, learn how to use the privacy settings. Unless you have a reason to reveal something to the world, restrict it to people you know and trust. Even then, don't post anything too sensitive. There are enough data breaches that anything you put online could go public.

STEP 4: Speaking of social media, wait until you get home to post those vacation photos—otherwise, you're announcing to burglars that your home is unattended. And resist the urge to answer public prompts for the kind of data you might use as a security code.

STEP 5: If you get a friend request from someone you already friended, there's a good chance it's a spoof account run by a scammer.

☐ If you've taken steps to protect your privacy, engrave your Social Security number on a victory trophy (but don't show it to anyone).

RICHER RISKS

Every financial decision, from the investments you make to the career you embark on, involves risk. You can't eliminate it. But you can understand and manage it.

UNDERSTAND PROBABILITIES

You can't truly understand risk if you don't understand probability. And many of us don't understand probability.

It's common to think "improbable" means impossible. In 2016, forecaster Nate Silver gave Donald Trump only a 29 percent chance of winning. When Trump won, some people thought it proved Silver was wrong. There's a 100 percent chance those people misunderstood how probability works.

Fortunately, there's a relatively easy way to get your head around probability. Research shows that when nonmathematicians think in terms of "times out of 100," it becomes easier to understand the odds.

STEP 1: If you're having trouble visualizing a probability, think of it as "number of times out of 100." If a researcher says there's a 1 percent chance of a company going bankrupt, interpret that as "Out of 100 companies like this one, one of them went broke."

STEP 2: Of course, some events don't actually repeat. Interpret "The Red Sox have a 20 percent chance of winning the World Series this year" as "If you could rewind time and run this series 100 times, the Sox would take twenty of them."

STEP 3: With that in mind, recognize that low-probability events will happen. If you go outside on ten days that have a 10 percent chance of rain, you'll probably get rained on once.

☐ If you've looked at probabilities as "times out of 100," give yourself a certain victory.

WATCH OUT FOR FALLACIES

Probabilistic thinking doesn't come naturally to humans. In our daily life, something happens or it doesn't. Fortunately, even if you aren't a mathematician, you can guard against some of the most common logical fallacies.

STEP 1: If a coin comes up heads ten times in a row, what are the odds that the next toss comes up heads, too? If you answered anything other than 50 percent, you fell victim to **the gambler's fallacy**. Coins don't have memories. But you do, so remember: Probabilities reset each time.

....

STEP 2: The opposite of the gambler's fallacy is **the hot-hand fallacy**—the belief that a lucky streak is destined to continue. If you hit the jackpot on a slot machine twice in a row, your odds of hitting another jackpot are just as low as they were if you'd never pulled the lever. Once again, remember: Probabilities reset every time.

....

STEP 3: If there's a low probability of something, it's human nature to act as if it can never happen. This is called **the appeal to probability,** and it's a fallacy, too. Guard against it by understanding probabilities as times out of 100 (previous page).

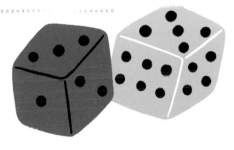

☐ If you've understood some of the most common fallacies about probability, you're due for a major victory.

RISK-BALANCE YOUR LIFE

The rest of this book is focused on using financial techniques to improve your finances. But I want to take a moment for a financial technique that you can apply to your entire life: **portfolio management**.

A good investor will think about the right balance of risk and safety in their investment portfolio (page 70). Why not be a good investor in your nonfinancial happiness, too?

STEP 1: Consider an area of your life where you want to maximize your return over a long period of time—say, the pleasure you get out of movies.

STEP 2: What are the safe options in that world? Can you always count on a superhero movie to entertain you, even if it's not especially profound?

STEP 3: What are the risky options in that world? For me, it's serious dramas. They might depress me. Or they might transform the way I see the world.

STEP 4: Think about the balance of risk and safety you'd like. Personally, I think 80/20 is a good mix when it comes to any art form—80 percent solid, predictable choices, 20 percent artistic risks.

STEP 5: Give yourself a rule of thumb (page 16) to make sure you stick with your asset allocation. Maybe you'll see action movies all summer long and then watch dramas all autumn. Maybe you'll make yourself see one serious film for every four explosion fests.

STEP 6: Whatever rule you set, try to stick with it for a few months. Then step back and see if it's made your life better. If not, tweak your risk/balance ratio based on what you've learned.

☐ If you've put together a risk portfolio in your nonfinancial life, it's a safe win.

HEDGE YOUR BETS

Diversification means reducing your overall risk by investing in lots of different things. **Hedging** means deliberately reducing your exposure to a specific risk.

Suppose I sell sunscreen by the seashore. To diversify, I might stock snacks and sundries.

But if I want to hedge specifically against the risk of bad weather, I might fill half my shelves with umbrellas. When the weather shifts from sun to rain, profits will drop on one of my lines, but rise on the other.

The good thing about hedging is that it protects you from all kinds of risk. The trade-off is that it prevents you from making as big a profit.

STEP 1: Identify a risk you're exposed to. What if there's a global healthy-eating trend, and the eccentric chocolate maker you work for has to close his magical factory?

STEP 2: Consider how you can hedge against it. Can you invest in your cousin James's giant-peach farm?

STEP 3: Think about the trade-off. By reducing your loss in a bad situation, you're reducing your gain in a great situation. Alas, there's no golden ticket. You'll have to decide if hedging will make you a champion of the world or just a twit.

☐ If you've hedged one risk, give yourself the win.

INSURE YOURSELF

From your life to your iPhone, there's no limit to the things you *could* insure. But what *should* you insure?

STEP 1: If you're debating whether to insure something, imagine things go wrong. What's the maximum it would realistically cost you?

STEP 2: Ask yourself: Would paying that cost result in a significant change in your financial circumstances?

STEP 3: If the answer is yes, insure yourself against it. Otherwise, don't bother. Do insure your $800,000 home. Don't insure your $30 headphones.

STEP 4: Don't forget to consider intangible risks, like the risk of a disabling injury that prevents you from working.

STEP 5: In borderline circumstances, consider setting aside money in a dedicated savings account, rather than giving it to the insurance company. For example, some pet owners would find a $7,000 vet bill unpleasant but just barely manageable. Rather than insure Megafloof, they might start setting aside a monthly sum when he's a healthy kitten so they're prepared when he reaches old age.

STEP 6: Make sure your policy would actually cover that maximum loss. Don't wait until your house burns down to discover that your policy only covers damage from meteorites.

STEP 7: Consider the maximum amount of money you can lose without feeling pain. Making that your deductible can reduce the cost of your insurance.

☐ If you've made a thoughtful decision about your insurance needs, you're guaranteed a win.

NEGATIVE HEDGE

Hedging reduces your risk and your potential rewards. **Negative hedging** is the reverse: It means increasing your risks to increase your rewards.

A negative hedge might simply involve betting more. Or it might involve investing in two stocks that are likely to move in parallel.

It's not a move I recommend often—but in certain very specific circumstances, it may be a good decision.

STEP 1: Are you very, very, very confident of an outcome? Consider a negative hedge to reap greater rewards. ("I just read about a company that invented calorie-free ice cream that cures cancer. I'm going to apply for a job with them—AND invest my life savings.")

STEP 2: If you're putting money aside for a specific purchase, are your savings useless if they don't reach a certain threshold? ("My brother is getting married tomorrow, an airline ticket to get there costs $500, and I've only got $250. I might as well risk it all at the roulette table.")

STEP 3: Do you care more about the thrill than the financial return? ("As a lifelong Red Sox fan, I've already bet my hopes and dreams on this year's series. If my buddy in New York is willing to put down ten bucks, I can make it even more exciting.")

STEP 4: Any time you negative-hedge, be very conscious of exactly how much you stand to lose, and make sure you can live with losing it. By definition, negative hedging is an all-in, high-risk technique.

☐ If you've engaged in a negative hedge, engage in a positive win.

RICHER
INVESTMENTS

This section is all about making your money work for you. As Ben Franklin once said, "Money makes money. And the money that money makes, makes money."

SAVE FOR A RAINY DAY

Sometimes, things go wrong. You might get fired. Your plumbing system might explode. In those cases, it helps to have a financial cushion.

But how much?

Many experts suggest you have enough savings to handle three to six months of expenses. That's good advice if you can swing it, but it ignores the financial realities of many people's lives. According to the Federal Reserve, nearly half of Americans would struggle to pay a single emergency expense of $400.

If three months of expenses seems like an impossible dream, don't despair. Economists Emily Gallagher and Jorge Sabat dived into the data and figured out which sums can be enough to prevent the disasters that keep people trapped in poverty. If you can reach any of those targets, you'll give your financial future a huge boost.

I should note that Gallagher and Sabat did their calculations in 2019 dollars. I've adjusted that for prices in 2022, when I'm writing this. By the time you read it, you may need a little more. You can search online for an inflation calculator and adjust from 2022 prices—or you can just bump all the numbers up a bit.

STEP 1: Add up all your monthly expenses. Multiply that by three (if your income is very dependable and you have a lot of expenses you could cut in an emergency), or six (if your income is less certain or your expenses are more fixed).

STEP 2: Could you reasonably save up that much money over the next year or two? If so, go ahead and start setting money aside. Even if you put only a little aside each month, it will add up.

STEP 3: If you can't reasonably save up that much money, pick a different target. $890 in savings is enough to prevent most families from having to skip meals if hardship strikes. $1,790 is enough to prevent a missed housing payment. $3,100 is enough to prevent missing regular bills. $3,150 is enough to prevent cutting back on medical treatment. Pick the lowest of these targets you can reach, and start saving. Once you reach that target, you can move on to the next one.

STEP 4: Whatever target you're reaching for, put the money into a savings account or other insured, easily accessible account. Don't invest it in anything risky!

☐ If you've started building up an emergency fund (or if you already have one), give yourself an emergency win.

FOLLOW THE MONEY

"Follow the money." In *All the President's Men*, that's how two reporters track a path of corruption all the way to the White House. Even if you're not trying to bring down a president, it's useful advice in your personal financial life.

STEP 1: Before you trust a reviewer or financial advisor, figure out how they make their money. Does that stockbroker get a commission when they sell you something? Is that article on how much insurance to buy published in a magazine that sells full-page ads to insurance companies?

STEP 2: Think about the incentives that method of payment creates. Anybody paid on commission is incentivized to sell you something, whether or not you'll really benefit from it. Anybody who needs advertising dollars has to keep their advertisers happy, whether or not that makes *you* happy.

STEP 3: When possible, seek out people whose financial incentives align with yours. That financial planner who gets a flat fee? She can't make extra money by selling you products you don't need. She *can* make extra money if her advice works out well for you and you come back to her again.

STEP 4: Don't entirely rule out somebody because of their incentives. A commission-based broker may genuinely believe in the stock she's selling you. An ad-filled magazine may have a strict policy of editorial integrity. But if the incentives are suspect, it's worth getting a second opinion before you act.

☐ If you've checked on somebody's financial incentives before you take their advice, buy a trophy from a company I have absolutely no connection to.

COMPARE PERCENTAGES

You've scrimped and saved all month, and you've ended with some spare cash to spend on your long-term financial future. Congratulations! But where should you put that money? A simple rule of thumb can help you find the greatest return on your investment.

STEP 1: If you don't yet have an adequate savings cushion (page 60), set aside money for that.

STEP 2: Make a list of your investment opportunities and debts. Include opportunities you haven't set up yet but could (like that IRA you've been meaning to get around to).

STEP 3: For debts, write down the annual interest rate the bank is getting. For savings accounts, write down the annual interest you're getting. For stocks, bonds, and mutual funds, write down their average annual rate of return over the longest past time frame you can find (or just write down 7 percent, the rough average return on a portfolio with 60 percent stocks and 40 percent bonds).

IRA (if I set it up): 10%
Mortgage: 6.34%
Savings account: 3%
Credit card debt: 21%
PAY THIS DOWN FIRST!

STEP 4: Put your money toward the highest interest rate on your list.

☐ If you've put money toward the place it will do you the greatest good, take a high-interest win.

PAY YOURSELF FIRST

If you're looking for a financial motto, "pay yourself first" is a great one. The idea is to send money winging toward your top financial priority before any shopkeeper, gadget salesman, or restaurateur can get their hands on it.

STEP 1: Identify your current top financial priority, whether that's paying off high-interest debt (page 82), building up a short-term savings cushion (page 60), or saving for a long-term goal (page 66).

STEP 2: When your paycheck comes in, set aside money for absolutely mandatory expenses, like your rent or mortgage. Then, before you spend on anything else, pay down your debt, deposit cash into a savings account, or invest toward your goal.

STEP 3: Even better, automate the process. Set up a direct deposit directly into your savings account, or a recurring transfer to pay down your debt.

☐ If you've paid yourself first, give yourself a win.

MAKE YOUR MONEY MAKE MONEY THAT MAKES MONEY

If you invest $100 at 10 percent interest, then you'll earn $10, and a year later, you'll have $110. That's fairly simple math.

Next year, you'll earn 10 percent on that $110, which is $11.10. You'll end up with $121.10, and next year, you'll earn interest on that. Thanks to the miracle of **compound interest**, you'll double your money in just over seven years.

I calculated that using a simple rule of thumb: **the rule of seventy-two**. To figure out roughly how long it takes for compound interest to double your money, just divide seventy-two by your interest rate. Seventy-two divided by 7 equals 10.3, so doubling your money at 7 percent interest will take about just over a decade.

Or to put it another way: At 7 percent interest, investing $10 today is as good as investing $20 in a decade, or $40 two decades from now.

If you don't want to bother with math, simply remember the Ben Franklin quote that began this section: "Money makes money. And the money that money makes, makes money."

Franklin's deeds lived up to his words. When he died in 1790, he left $5,000 to Boston and Philadelphia, to compound for two hundred years (with a $500,000 withdrawal after a century). In 1991, the two cities split about $4 million.

You might not be able to let your money compound for two centuries, but the sooner you start investing, the more work compound interest will do for you.

STEP 1: If you have high-interest debt, then compound interest is working against you. Make paying it down a priority (page 82).

STEP 2: Otherwise, identify a long-term investment goal, and remember that the sooner you start working toward it, the longer your money can compound.

STEP 3: If you're investing in a savings account, make sure it pays interest on your interest, not just on the original amount. If you're investing in a stock and you don't need the returns right away, sign up for dividend reinvestment to make sure any cash you get is plowed back into the stock.

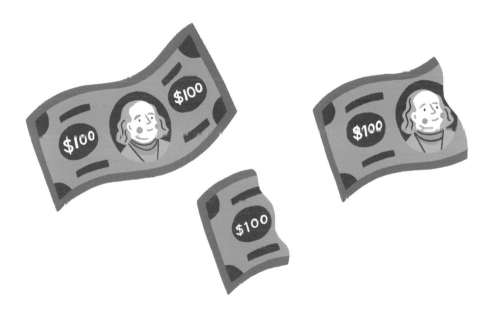

☐ If you've set your money compounding today, instead of waiting for the future, you've earned 100 percent of a win.

AN INVESTMENT YOU CAN LIVE IN

If you buy stock in a company and it goes out of business, your shares won't do you much good. But if you buy a house, even if prices crash, you still have a place to live. If you don't already own your own home, here are the first steps to get on the ladder.

STEP 1: Find an online rent vs. buy calculator and check if buying a house is the best option for your specific financial circumstances.

STEP 2: More importantly than its investment value, a house is a tool for living a better life. Consider your core values (page 5). If flexibility and freedom are more important than stability, you might be better off renting.

STEP 3: Consider how long you would realistically live in this property. If it's less than 5 to 7 years, it's unlikely to be worth the money.

STEP 4: If you still want to buy, find out your credit score (page 89). Do what you can to improve it (page 94). The better it is, the more likely you are to be approved for a mortgage on good terms.

> **My gross monthly income: $3,000**
>
> 0.36 x $3,000 = $1,080
>
> Student loan payment: $370
>
> Maximum monthly mortgage:
> $1,080-$370 = $710

STEP 5: The amount a bank will lend you depends on your credit score, your down payment, and your savings. But for a rough estimate, take 36 percent of the money you make before taxes and other deductions. Then subtract any monthly debt payments you already have. What's left is the maximum monthly mortgage payment (including taxes and insurance) you're likely to have approved.

STEP 6: The maximum you might get isn't the maximum you *should* get. Think about what you can genuinely afford, given your monthly expenses. Remember to include the new expenses you'll have as a homeowner, like homeowner's insurance, property taxes, repairs, etc.

STEP 7: Once you've come up with a realistic monthly amount, find an online mortgage calculator and figure out how much of a total mortgage that works out to. Playing around with different down payments, and comparing the results with prices in your area, will give you an idea of how much you need to save.

STEP 8: Start saving for a down payment. If you're going to buy a home within the next year or two, keep it in something safe like a savings account. Otherwise, invest appropriately for your time frame.

STEP 9: More than half of first-time home buyers need financial help from family and friends. Don't be embarrassed to ask for help. And don't assume your friends who already own homes are smarter or harder working than you. They may have external resources that you don't.

STEP 10: While you're saving for a down payment, start saving documents, too. A lender may want to see a month or two of pay stubs, two years of taxes, up to six months of bank statements, and information on any savings or retirement accounts you have. Putting all these documents together slowly over time is less stressful than rushing to assemble them at the last minute.

STEP 11: If you're self-employed, a lender may base their loan on your adjusted gross income from Schedule C (Form 1040) of your taxes. It may be worth taking fewer deductions in the two years before you buy your house, even if you end up paying taxes on a higher income.

> ☐ If you've taken the first steps to owning your own home (or if you're already a homeowner), feel at home in victory.

STOCKS VS. BONDS

When you buy **stock**, you become part owner of a company. As an owner, you could make vast profits or lose everything, depending on how the company does.

When you buy a **bond**, you're essentially loaning money to a company or a government. As long as they don't go bankrupt, you'll get your money back, plus interest. The more reliable the borrower is, the less interest they'll pay you.

All that makes bonds a great tool for managing risk. But as always with investment, there's a trade-off between risk and reward. Broadly, the longer it is before you'll cash out your investments, the more risks you can take, and the greater percentage of your money you can invest in stocks.

(Note that these rules apply only to long-term investing; your short-term emergency fund (page 60) should be in a savings account or something equally safe.)

Stocks Vs. Bonds

STOCKS	BONDS
• Give partial ownership of the company.	• Give partial ownership of a debt.
• Can fluctuate wildly in value.	• Have a specific "maturity" date, at which point you can cash them in for a specified amount.
• May result in dividends, depending on how the company does.	• If you want to sell the bond before the maturity date, the value could rise and fall. But unless the borrower defaults on the loan, you know in advance what they'll be worth on the maturity date.
• Don't have a specific end date; you hold them until you choose to sell them, or the company goes bust.	

STEP 1: Subtract your age from 120. That's the percentage of an investment portfolio that an average person should invest in stocks. For example, if you're thirty, you should invest 90 percent in stocks and 10 percent in bonds or cash.

STEP 2: Think about your tolerance for risk.

STEP 3: If you're a cautious, play-it-safe type, invest in fewer stocks and more bonds or cash. If you're a go-for-broke risk devotee, invest in more stocks. Some advisors suggest cautious investors subtract their age from 100 and high-risk types subtract it from 130.

STEP 4: Adjust your portfolio as the years go by to make sure the mix stays roughly right for your age.

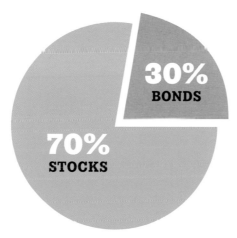

A middle-of-the-road fifty-year-old.

☐ If you've thought about how much risk you want to take in balancing stocks and bonds, take a well-balanced win.

BUY AN INDEX FUND

A massive analysis of the stock market from 1926 through 2016 found something surprising:

If you had bought every single stock for ninety years, you only would have made a gain on the top 4 percent of stocks. The other 96 percent collectively did no better than holding low-risk treasury certificates—and many of them did much worse.

> ## There are three strategies you might consider in response to that information:
>
> 1. Try to zoom in on that 4 percent by picking a handful of stocks you understand deeply (page 74).
>
> 2. Trust a portfolio manager to actively sort through stocks, buying winners and selling losers.
>
> 3. Don't try to pick stocks; just own lots of them, raising the odds that you'll stumble onto some of that 4 percent.

Strategy 1 has potentially huge returns, but equally big risks. I talk about it on page 74.

Strategy 2 sounds like it should work—but over a ten-year period, more than 85 percent of managed funds underperform the market.

That's why many people turn to **index funds**. A stock index is a list of stocks based on some common principles; an index fund is just a collection of stocks in a particular index. For example, a committee at Standard & Poor's chooses about five hundred stocks to be representative of big American corporations and calls that list the S&P 500. An S&P 500 index fund contains shares in all the stocks in the S&P 500, in rough proportion to their size.

STEP 1: When you invest money in the stock market, be very skeptical of any fund manager who claims they can beat the market.

STEP 2: If you don't have exceptional reason to trust a fund manager, consider investing in an index fund instead.

STEP 3: If you're confident about a particular industry or region, you can find an index that tracks it. Otherwise, you might be better off with an index that tracks stocks generally in your country, or even the world.

☐ If you've invested in an index fund, add a victory to your portfolio.

DON'T DIVERSIFY

Conventional wisdom is to diversify your portfolio by investing in a wide range of stocks (page 72). But I feel obligated to tell you that Warren Buffett, one of the richest men in the world, got there by doing the opposite.

Buffett is a proponent of **focus investing**—placing bets on a small handful of carefully chosen stocks. Within that small portfolio, it's good to have a diversity of industries. You might hold a carefully researched food company, a carefully researched technology company, and a carefully researched insurance company. But that's a far cry from the hundreds of stocks you might hold in an index fund.

To learn more about focus investing, read *The Warren Buffett Way* by Robert G. Hagstrom.

It's not an approach for most people—again, 85 percent of full-time investment professionals underperform the market. But if you've got the patience and self-confidence for focus investing, it's an approach with potentially vast returns.

Is Focus Investing Right for You?

Successful focus investors:

- Hold their investments between three years and forever.
- Are comfortable doing math.
- Trust their own judgment.
- Have a high tolerance for risk.
- Can handle the stressful swings in value that focused portfolios are subject to.

STEP 1: Ask yourself if you're suited to be a focus investor (see sidebar).

STEP 2: Do a deep dive on a company you admire. Download years of annual reports. Look at assets, income, and expenses.

STEP 3: Do a deep dive on the industry the company is in. Is it likely to exist in a decade? Does this company have some unique advantage within that industry?

STEP 4: Now do a deep dive on the company's leadership. Are they rational? Do they focus on long-term shareholder value, rather than next week's stock price? Do they make decisions based on the unique needs of their company or just follow trends?

STEP 5: Given what you know about the company, what would a fair price be for a share in it? If the stock price is a good value, buy it.

STEP 6: Hang on to it for years. Only sell it when you need the money, the business fundamentals change, or an even better long-term investment opportunity presents itself.

STEP 7: If you don't have the stomach for full-on focus investing, consider a hybrid approach. Personally, when I make an investment, it's usually in index funds, but on very rare occasions, if I feel I understand a business particularly well, I make a focus-style bet.

☐ If you've done a deep dive into a company and considered a focused investment, focus on your win.

BUY AND SELL AS RARELY AS POSSIBLE

Those of us who don't have the stomach for focus investing (page 74) would still do well to remember a key piece of wisdom from Warren Buffett: "The stock market is designed to transfer money from the active to the patient."

The more often you buy and sell, the more commissions and trading fees you might pay. If you hold stocks for less than a year before selling them, you pay short-term capital gains taxes, which are higher than long-term. And thanks to the miracle of compound interest (page 66), those small present-day losses can add up to massive future ones.

Plus, human judgment is fallible, and fidgety investors often buy and sell at the wrong time. One study found that the best performing investment accounts belonged to people who forgot they had them and never made any trades!

STEP 1: Before you buy a stock, ask yourself: If you weren't allowed to sell it for the next couple of years, would you still buy it?

. . . .

STEP 2: Once you've purchased a stock, don't sell it without a good reason. "Selling it now is part of my long-term plan" is a good reason. So is "I need the money to feed my family" or "The company's long-term prospects have fundamentally changed." But "I'm trying to time the market" and "I'm bored" are not.

☐ If you've left your investments alone, actively take the win.

GIVE FUTURE YOU A RAISE

The only thing better than a sudden windfall is a regular salary increase. But why should Present-Day You be the only one to enjoy your good fortune? Using the extra cash to increase your savings is like giving a raise to all the Future Yous as well.

STEP 1: If you get an unexpected windfall, and you don't have high-interest debts or other pressing expenses, let yourself spend a small percentage as mad money, but save the rest.

STEP 2: If you've been saving 10 percent of your income, and you get a raise, save at least 10 percent of that new amount, too. In fact, consider raising your savings even faster than you're raising your income; if you've been getting by on your old income, getting by on your old income plus half your raise will still be a boost.

☐ If you've increased the rate at which you save to match a raise you just got, increase your number of wins by one.

CUT YOUR ENDOWMENT

Imagine a coffee mug with a charming picture of your favorite place. How much would you pay for it?

Now imagine that you already own this mug. How much would I have to pay you to give it up?

From an economic point of view, the answer should be the same to both questions. If the mug is worth ten bucks, then it's worth ten bucks whether you're buying or selling. But most people need more money to give up something they already have.

Psychologists call this **the endowment effect**—our tendency to value stuff we already have, simply because we have it. It may be caused by **loss aversion**—the fact that the pain of loss is greater than the pleasure of an equivalent gain.

When it comes to mugs, loss aversion and the endowment effect are amusing curiosities. When it comes to investments, they can be serious financial hazards.

STEP 1: Consider an investment you already have, like the 100 shares of American Horse & Buggy Incorporated you inherited from your grandparents.

STEP 2: See how much money you could get for it.

STEP 3: Suppose you didn't own it already and I offered to sell it to you at the current price. Would you consider that a good deal? Do you really think the horse and buggy industry is poised for massive growth?

STEP 4: If the answer is no, it's probably time to sell.

STEP 5: Next time you're in a situation where things may go wrong, guard against loss aversion by setting up a rule of thumb in advance. For example, "As soon as I'm down by $100, I will walk away from the poker table."

> ☐ If you've taken steps to avoid the endowment effect or loss aversion, it's a win.

DECLUTTER FOR PROFIT

If you need more space in your home, there are two approaches. One is to rent a storage unit for your extra stuff. That costs money. The other is to sell your extra stuff. That makes money. Guess which I recommend?

STEP 1: Think about the items in your house you don't regularly use. Which one do you think has the highest resale value?

STEP 2: Search the web to learn what people are paying for on sales site like Facebook Marketplace or an auction site like eBay. Search for items that actually sold. Just because some optimistic seller is asking $50 for "vintage toilet paper" doesn't mean buyers will pay that much.

STEP 3: Find out how much commission the website charges, and subtract it from the sales price. That's the amount you might walk away with.

STEP 4: To help you overcome the endowment effect (page 78), try a thought experiment. Imagine I offer you two boxes. One has a T-shirt exactly like the one you bought at an Andrew W.K. concert in 2002. The other has the $5.80 you could get from selling it. Which box do you take? If you choose the cash, it's time to sell.

☐ If you've sold one unwanted item, buy a win.

RICHER
CREDIT

Debt is a valuable financial tool. Governments use it to finance interstate highways. Individuals use it to finance homes. But any tool can be dangerous if not used properly. This chapter will help you use credit to build up your financial security, rather than tear it down.

PAY DOWN HIGH-INTEREST DEBT

Secured debt—borrowing money to buy a home or other valuable asset—can make your life better. But **unsecured debt**—like credit card purchases or payday loans—is often a far worse deal. Too much debt in general (and unsecured debt in particular) has been linked to greater stress and poorer health.

Credit cards are especially dangerous because they make it so easy to take on more debt at a very high interest rate. If you pay off your credit card bills every month, great! You can skip this entry. But if you've got high-interest debt, make paying it down your priority.

STEP 1: Make a list of all the money you owe.

STEP 2: Find the interest rate for each loan.

STEP 3: To avoid penalty charges, make the minimum monthly payment on every credit card or loan you have.

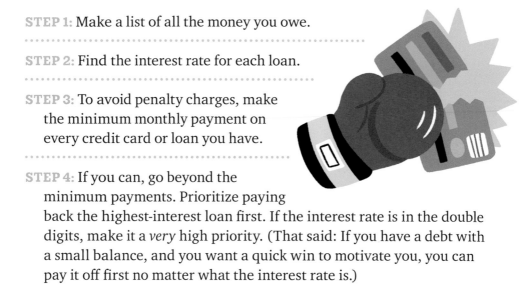

STEP 4: If you can, go beyond the minimum payments. Prioritize paying back the highest-interest loan first. If the interest rate is in the double digits, make it a *very* high priority. (That said: If you have a debt with a small balance, and you want a quick win to motivate you, you can pay it off first no matter what the interest rate is.)

STEP 5: If your debt feels overwhelming, or you're not sure where to begin, a nonprofit credit counselor can help you work out a plan. See page 92 for tips.

☐ If you've reduced your high-interest debt, increase your tally of wins.

KNOW THE FULL COST

Which costs less: a car loan with a $700 monthly payment or one with a $600 monthly payment?

It's a trick question. Unless you know how long the loan will last, you can't calculate the total cost.

STEP 1: When considering a loan, make sure you can afford the monthly payments, given all your other expenses.

. . . .

STEP 2: Find out how many months you'll be making those payments, and multiply that by your monthly payment. The result is your total out-of-pocket expense. A $600-per-month loan that takes six years to repay will set you back $43,200.

. . . .

STEP 3: Compare that loan cost to the price of buying the thing in cash. If that $43,200 loan is for a $40,000 car, you're paying an extra $3,200 for the privilege of paying in installments. If you need the car and you don't have that much cash, it might well be worth it—but if you can get a cheaper car and borrow less, you can put more money in your pocket and less in the bank's.

☐ If you've figured out the true cost of a loan, take a win on credit.

APPRECIATE APPRECIATION

Let's go back to the car loan we talked about on the previous page. As you'll remember, after six years, you ended up paying $43,200 for a $40,000 car.

But there's a catch. The car was worth only forty grand when it was sitting at the dealership. The instant you drove it off the lot, it began to **depreciate**, or lose value. By the time you've paid off your loan, your car might be worth about $23,000.

By contrast, if you buy a house, it may well **appreciate**, or gain value. If you take out a thirty-year mortgage on a $400,000 home, you might end up paying $800,000. But if your home appreciates 7 percent a year, then by the time you make your final payment it would be worth more than $3 million.

Paying $800,000 for something worth $3 million is a great deal. Paying $43,200 for something worth $23,000 is a lousy deal. That's why, as a rough rule of thumb, you should borrow money only to buy things that will appreciate.

STEP 1: If you're tempted to buy something on credit, figure out what it's likely to be worth at the end of the loan period. Search the web for "car depreciation calculator," or check used-car sites to find out what people are currently paying for a three-year-old Honda.

STEP 2: Add in any extra value the purchase will give you. If you can take the bus to a job that pays $20,000 but could drive to a job that pays $30,000, then the car is worth an extra ten grand per year.

STEP 3: Subtract any extra costs that come with the purchase. If you can get a bus pass for $500 a year, and driving will cost you $1,500 annually in gas and insurance, then subtract $1,000 from the value of the car.

STEP 4: Compare the final value of the thing to the initial value. Is it going to appreciate or depreciate? If it's going to depreciate, and you can get by without it, don't borrow money to get it.

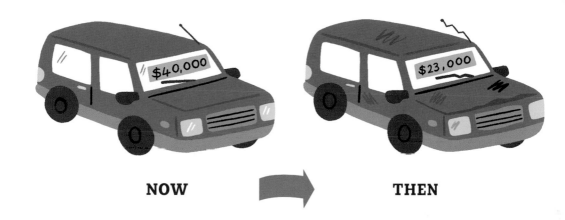

NOW ➡ **THEN**

NOW ➡ **THEN**

☐ If you've thought about whether something will depreciate before you've taken out a loan, appreciate your victory.

START FROM SCRATCH

Building up a good credit history is simple: Make your loan payments every month.

Getting a loan is simple: Have a good credit history.

Sensing a paradox? Don't worry: Everybody starts their credit history from zero. If that's where you are, here are some steps you can take to build it up. These come from writer/editor Penelope Wang of *Consumer Reports*.

STEP 1: If you don't have a checking account, set one up.

STEP 2: Consider a **secured credit card**. You put down a deposit that becomes your credit card limit. If you don't pay your bills, the bank can take the deposit. That means you'll want to be careful about not spending more than you can afford! But it also means the bank won't need to see an extensive credit record before giving you the card. If you're not sure where to apply for one, you can start with the bank where you've got your checking account.

STEP 3: Pay the full balance on your secured credit card consistently, and the bank will eventually refund your deposit and offer you an unsecured card.

STEP 4: Alternatively, consider a **credit-builder loan**. If you borrow, say, $500 on one of these loans, the bank sets aside $500 in a savings account. You get access to it when you've fully paid off the loan. Banks will usually charge interest on the loan as well as a fee, so you end up paying for the privilege of building up your credit score. Shop around to get the best deal.

STEP 5: If you pay money to anybody regularly—whether the gas company or your landlord—ask them to report your payments to credit bureaus.

☐ If you've taken some the first steps to build a good credit record, take a win on credit.

SHOP FOR PERKS

If you've got good credit, banks are eager to lend you money. So eager, in fact, that they may pay *you* for the privilege. Find a credit card with good perks and it's like getting a small discount off every purchase you make.

STEP 1: Shop around to see what credit card offers are out there. Your bank and your existing credit cards are good places to start.

STEP 2: Figure out roughly how much each perk is worth to you per year. If it will take you two years to build up enough frequent-flier points for a $500 ticket, the perks are worth $250 annually.

STEP 3: Subtract the annual fee from the value of the perks. That's the annual value of the card . . . in theory.

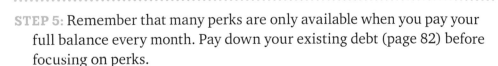

STEP 4: Think about any restrictions you'll face when you try to cash in your points. $200 in hassle-free store vouchers may be better than $250 in airline miles you can only use for off-peak travel to Siberia.

STEP 5: Remember that many perks are only available when you pay your full balance every month. Pay down your existing debt (page 82) before focusing on perks.

☐ If you've found a credit card that pays you to use it, your perk is a victory.

READ ALL ABOUT YOU

Whether you're applying for a store credit card or a mortgage, potential lenders are going to see your credit report. You should see it, too. It gives you insight into an important aspect of your financial health, and it can help you catch identity fraud.

 To learn more, go to **usa.gov/credit-reports**

STEP 1: Go to **AnnualCreditReport.com**.

STEP 2: Request a credit report from each credit agency on the site. You can do this once a year at no charge.

STEP 3: Read through your credit reports carefully. Are there transactions, loans, or addresses you don't recognize? If so, you may be the victim of identity fraud (page 48).

STEP 4: If there are mistakes on the report, dispute them. Learn how at **consumer.ftc.gov/articles/disputing-errors-your-credit-reports**.

STEP 5: If your report isn't great, don't stress. A bad credit report isn't forever. Bankruptcy can only be reported for ten years, and most other bad news for seven. See the rest of this chapter for tips on repairing things in the meantime.

☐ If you've checked your credit report, give yourself an A+.

CREDIT REPORT A+

REFINANCE

If you've got an outstanding loan and you can reduce the interest rate, it's like free money. Admittedly, it's free money that may have an upfront fee and probably comes with a ton of terms and conditions. But once you get past that: free money. What could be better?

STEP 1: Look at your outstanding loans.

....

STEP 2: For each kind of loan, find comparable interest rates. If you have a mortgage, what are lenders offering nowadays? If you have outstanding credit card debt, are there cards that will let you transfer your existing balance at a lower rate? If you have student loans, are they private (ideal for refinancing) or are they federal loans that would qualify for some sort of forgiveness (not ideal for refinancing)?

STEP 3: If the rates are lower, figure out how much you could save each month.

STEP 4: Find out how much it will cost to switch. Your new lender might charge you handling fees, and your old one might charge you for early repayment. If you're switching credit cards, the new one may charge a transfer fee, based on the balance you're transferring. They might also have a higher annual fee.

STEP 5: Don't be fooled by "introductory offers." Who cares if a credit card gives you 0 percent interest for two months, if it then switches you to a rate that's even worse than your current one?

STEP 6: Take time to do the math. Add up the savings and subtract the fees. If the new loan will save you more than it costs over the next few years, it's probably worth switching.

☐ If you've refinanced one loan, start collecting interest on a victory.

HIGH INTEREST

LOW INTEREST

GET A GOOD CREDIT COUNSELOR

If you're overwhelmed by the amount you owe, or you just can't figure out how to climb out of debt on your own, it's worth reaching out to a nonprofit credit counselor. Depending on your situation, they can help you negotiate a repayment schedule with your debtors or possibly declare personal bankruptcy.

But make sure you do your homework first. You don't want to end up with an unqualified counselor or one who has financial incentives to steer you toward a particular option.

Questions to Ask

- What services do you offer?
- Do you offer information? Are educational materials available for free?
- Besides helping me solve my immediate problem, will you help me develop a plan for avoiding problems in the future?
- What are your fees?
- What if I can't afford to pay your fees or make contributions?
- Will I have a formal written agreement or contract with you?
- Are you licensed to offer your services in my state?
- What are the qualifications of your counselors? Are they accredited or certified by an outside organization? If so, by whom? If not, how are they trained? Try to use an organization whose counselors are trained by a nonaffiliated party.
- What assurance do I have that information about me (including my address, phone number, and financial information) will be kept confidential and secure?
- Do your employees get paid more or less depending on what they persuade me to do?

To learn more about bankruptcy, debt, and credit counseling, go to **consumer.ftc.gov/articles/0153-choosing-credit-counselor/**. (URLs change all the time, so if that's no longer valid, just go to **consumer.ftc.gov** and browse for the info you want.)

STEP 1: Find a nonprofit credit counselor. You can get help from your local credit union, religious organization, or nonprofit organization.

STEP 2: When you speak to a counselor, ask the questions on page 92, which come courtesy of the Federal Trade Commission. Get all the answers in writing.

STEP 3: Avoid organizations that display any of the following warning signs:

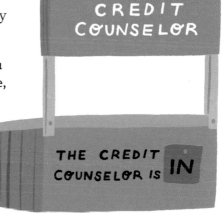

- Their employees get paid more if you sign up for certain services, pay a fee, or make a donation.

- They push you toward a debt management program before they thoroughly analyze your specific situation.

- They won't help you if you can't afford to pay.

- They won't put everything they tell you in writing.

- They charge for information or educational materials.

- They encourage you to stop paying your debts, put the money in a savings account, and then try to use it for a lump-sum settlement. There's no guarantee your debtors will accept the deal, and you can wreck your credit rating in the process.

☐ If you worked with a credit counselor (or even took steps toward getting one), credit yourself with a win.

IMPROVE YOUR SCORE

Knowing your credit score (page 89) is an important first step. But knowledge is only half the battle. If your score is lower than you want it to be, here are steps you can take to improve it, according to the Federal Deposit Insurance Company (the government agency that keeps the nation's financial system stable).

STEP 1: Your payment history is 35 percent of your score. Make payments on time, including medical bills that go into collections.

STEP 2: 30 percent of your score is based on how much of your credit limit is in use. Pay down your debt (page 82), and stick within your credit limit. Using less than 30 percent of your available credit can bump up your score significantly.

STEP 3: The *length* of your credit history is 15 percent of your total score. If you've got a long-standing account, pay it down but don't close it.

STEP 4: Be judicious about starting new credit accounts. Opening too many in a short period of time can lower your score.

STEP 5: Having a diverse **credit mix** improves your score, because it shows you can handle different types of credit. Over time, you want to accumulate a mix of **revolving credit accounts** (like credit cards) and **installment loans** (like auto loans or student loans). But this is only 10 percent of your score; getting more loans than you can repay will do you more harm than good.

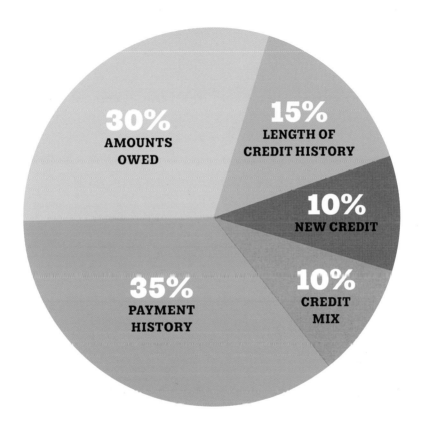

30%
AMOUNTS OWED

15%
LENGTH OF CREDIT HISTORY

10%
NEW CREDIT

35%
PAYMENT HISTORY

10%
CREDIT MIX

☐ If you've taken steps to improve your credit score, improve your number of wins.

FREEZE YOUR CREDIT CARDS

It's hard enough to pay down high-interest debt (page 82). The last thing you want to do is add more on top of it.

STEP 1: If you pay off your credit card balances in full every month, great! You can skip the rest of this entry.

STEP 2: If you're running a balance on any card, take it out of your wallet and lock it in a drawer. Or put it in a container, fill it with water, and stash it in the back of your freezer. You'll still be able to access it in an emergency, but it'll be out of reach for ordinary temptations.

STEP 3: If you have your credit card information stored in a browser, digital wallet, or website, delete it.

STEP 4: If you don't want to give up the convenience of credit cards, you can get a debit card that deducts money directly from your bank account. Or—if you're worried you'll lose track of spending and accidentally empty your bank account— you can also buy debit cards with a prepaid balance.

☐ If you've cut up or disabled a credit card, piece together a win.

RICHER SPENDING

As important as it is to save and invest, you can't take it with you. The ultimate goal of money is to make your life better, so spend it wisely. This chapter will show you how.

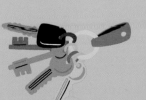

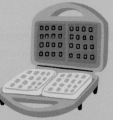

KNOW YOUR DISCOUNTS

There's never a reason to spend more than you have to. Knowing what discounts you qualify for is like having an infinitely reusable coupon.

STEP 1: See if your employer offers discounts with any retailers through its employee reward program.

STEP 2: Some companies offer discounts to certain professions, like educators, members of the military, government employees, or clergy. Whatever you do, if you're making a major purchase, it's worth asking if you qualify.

STEP 3: If you're a member of any organization, from the American Automobile Association to the Zydeco Zebras, check its website to see what discounts you're eligible for.

STEP 4: Install an extension in your web browser that will suggest discount codes on checkout. To avoid malware, make sure you get it from the official extension site run by your browser manufacturer.

STEP 5: If all else fails, ask, "Is this the best price you can give me?" The worst the salesperson can do is say, "Yes."

☐ If you've gotten a discount, take 10 percent off a victory trophy.

THINK ABOUT TUESDAY

If your kitchen is stocked with useless gadgets, from a microwaveable s'more maker to a specialized asparagus peeler, you may be guilty of **focalism**.

Focalism is the psychological tendency to focus on a hypothetical event, rather than the overall flow of your life. When you saw that s'more maker on sale, you thought about how joyfully you would use it, not how rarely.

A simple exercise, suggested by Elizabeth Dunn and Michael Norton in their book *Happy Money*, can help you stay focalism-free.

To learn more, read *Happy Money* by Elizabeth Dunn and Michael Norton.

STEP 1: When you are tempted to make a purchase, ask yourself how it would fit into your life on a specific day—say, next Tuesday.

STEP 2: Get out your calendar and dive into the specifics. Are you really going to come home from a long day at work and start peeling asparagus?

STEP 3: If you aren't going to use the purchase on this specific day, ask yourself: Why should any other day be different?

☐ If you've used the Next Tuesday test to fend off focalism, focus on your win.

BE TEMPTED LATER

When you really, really want something, the thought that you'll never get it can seem unbearable. It hurts too much to think, "I may never buy that solid-gold tofu spoon," so you go ahead and buy it.

Fortunately, there's an alternative. Psychologists call it **unspecific postponement**, and studies show it's an effective way to resist temptation.

STEP 1: When you're tempted to splurge on something you know you don't need, don't buy it now, but don't give up on it forever. Just tell yourself, "I'll buy it some other time."

STEP 2: Next time the urge occurs, tell yourself the same thing. This should become easier over time; studies suggest that the more you postpone temptation, the less it will tempt you.

☐ If you've put off one splurge to an unspecified future date, don't put off celebrating your win.

ELIMINATE THE MIDDLE MAN

Travel websites like Expedia and apps like Uber Eats are massive conveniences. But you pay for that convenience. Whether or not there's a delivery charge, third-party websites frequently pad their prices to make their profit. One study found that ordering takeout through a third-party app costs an extra 23 percent. And because third-party websites can take big commissions, the businesses they broker would love to deal with you directly. Those businesses will frequently express their joy through even bigger discounts.

STEP 1: If you're ordering delivery, order directly from the restaurant, rather than a third party. While you're at it, ask if the restaurant offers a discount for pickup; you may find that venturing out of your house can save you more than enough to pay for the gas.

STEP 2: If you're booking a hotel through a third-party website like Expedia or Travelocity, call the hotel directly. Tell them the rate you've found online, and ask if they can beat it—or at least match it and throw in a few extra perks.

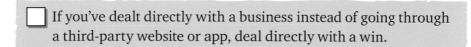

☐ If you've dealt directly with a business instead of going through a third-party website or app, deal directly with a win.

THE INCREDIBLE BULK

Bulk buying can get you bulk savings. But approach it thoughtfully; bulk impulse buying brings bulk problems.

STEP 1: Find a store near you that sells items in bulk.

STEP 2: Before you're tempted by a pallet full of deals, check how much storage space you've got. Then think about the products you go through most quickly. Write down the things you'd most like to buy in bulk.

STEP 3: Once you're roaming the aisles, open up the calculator in your phone. Divide the cost of the package by the number of items to figure out if you're really getting a good deal. Stores are not above putting up signs that say, SPECIAL! 1 CANDY BAR FOR 99 CENTS. 10 CANDY BARS FOR ONLY 10 DOLLARS!

STEP 4: Consider how long it will take you to go through a big volume of the product. Do you really want to store that industrial-size vat of popcorn for the next decade?

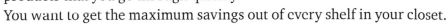

STEP 5: If you have limited storage room, prioritize long-lasting, compact products that you go through quickly. You want to get the maximum savings out of every shelf in your closet.

STEP 6: If it's a good deal, and you've got the space for it . . . bulk up.

☐ If you've bought something in bulk (and checked that it really is a better deal), give yourself ten thousand victories.

SKIP THE PACKAGE

Bulk purchases are often cheaper (previous page), but you can end up with more than you need. Smaller sizes are more convenient, but the extra cost can add up.

If you can find a shop that sells packaging-free bulk foods, you may be able to get the best of both worlds. At my local bulk-food store, for example, prices are about 10 percent cheaper than at my local supermarket. As a bonus, buying exactly the amount you need reduces your risk of food waste, which is good for your wallet—and by taking your own packaging, you help cut down on single-use plastic, which is good for the earth.

STEP 1: Search for "bulk food," "zero waste," or "packaging free" stores near you.

STEP 2: Take your own containers, shop, and save.

STEP 3: If you have a food allergy, be extra careful, since cross-contamination is more likely when things aren't sealed individually.

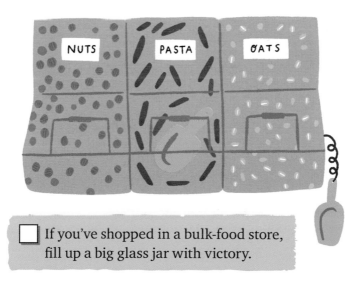

☐ If you've shopped in a bulk-food store, fill up a big glass jar with victory.

BUY LOTS OF LITTLE THINGS

Setting small amounts of money aside for a big investment: wise and mature.

Setting small amounts of money aside for a big splurge: surprisingly self-defeating.

Why? A psychological principal called **hedonic adaptation**. If you buy an expensive new coat, you'll feel a flurry of excitement, but it will soon fade, returning you to your previous emotional state. If you buy a fun new pair of socks every week, you get a smaller thrill from each purchase—but as each thrill fades, you can replace it with a new one. The result: longer-lasting and ultimately greater fun for the same amount of money.

STEP 1: Identify an amount of money you can afford to spend on fun stuff.

STEP 2: Instead of using it on one big thing, spend it on a bunch of little ones. Divide it by twelve, and get yourself a new hardback book every month. Or divide it by fifty-two, and get yourself an unnecessarily fancy pastry every Friday.

☐ If you've spent money you can afford on a series of small pleasures, enjoy a series of wins.

BUY MEMORIES, NOT THINGS

You buy an inexpensive new handbag. It's not very exciting, but unlike your old one, it doesn't have holes in it. Your happiness level increases…

…until the plain, utilitarian fabric of your new purse begins to annoy you as much as the holes in the old one did. So you buy a colorful cloth handbag, and your happiness level goes up again…until you begin to crave an elegantly understated leather purse.

It's another example of hedonic adaptation (previous page): the human tendency to get tired of things we once might have dreamed of. The good news is that we don't get tired of memories the same way we get tired of physical stuff. That means that money spent on experiences is much less likely to trap you in an endlessly expensive cycle of upgrades.

STEP 1: Think about money you planned to spend on an object that would make you happy.

STEP 2: Find a way to spend that money on a happy experience. Instead of a solar-powered, ergonomic bottle opener, buy a bottle of wine, open it the old-fashioned way, and share it with a friend.

⬜ If you've bought an experience instead of a thing or enjoyed a happy memory for free, experience a win.

MAKE A ONE-NUMBER BUDGET

A budget is a valuable tool for bridging the divide between good intentions and good real-world decisions. And it doesn't have to be complicated.

STEP 1: Figure out what your monthly take-home pay is, after taxes.

STEP 2: Add up your **fixed expenses**, including mandatory stuff like rent or your mortgage, and optional recurring stuff like your gym membership.

STEP 3: If your fixed expenses don't include a way of paying yourself first (page 65), fix that! Set up an automatic transfer to a savings account, retirement plan, or other investment account.

STEP 4: Subtract your fixed expenses from your monthly pay. That's how much flexible money you have to play with each month.

STEP 5: Divide your monthly flexible money by 4.3 (the average number of weeks in a month) to get your **weekly flexible spending budget.**

FLEXIBLE SPENDING

FIXED EXPENSES

STEP 6: Track your weekly spending. You don't have to write every purchase down—you could just pick a single credit card that you put all your optional purchases on. (Practice good credit hygiene: Don't carry a monthly balance.)

STEP 7: Before you make a purchase, check your weekly balance to see how much you've got left at your weekly budget.

STEP 8: Check in with yourself at the end of every month. Were on you target?

☐ If you've worked out (or stuck with) a one-number budget, you're number one!

MAKE A MANY-NUMBER BUDGET

If you need more precision than a one-number budget provides, or if you just love diving into the details, you can make a more traditional budget.

STEP 1: Make a list of all the things you spend money on. For most people, that would include: housing, food, insurance, entertainment, transportation, savings, and clothing. Depending on your lifestyle, it might also include childcare, medical expenses, or life-size reproductions of Michelangelo's *David*. You may want to throw in a "Miscellaneous" category for random other stuff.

STEP 2: Figure out how much money you take home each month, after taxes and other deductions.

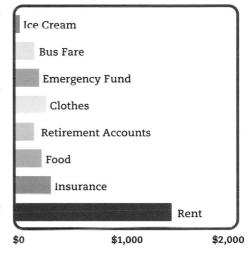

STEP 3: Decide how much you want to spend every month on each category. If your total spending adds up to more than your take-home pay, you need to rethink.

STEP 4: Track your spending (page 108), and compare it with your budget. If the numbers don't match up, think about why. Was your budget unrealistic? Or is your spending out of whack with your priorities?

STEP 5: Adjust your spending or your budget accordingly.

☐ If you've worked out (or stuck to) a detailed budget, budget in a victory.

TRACK YOUR SPENDING

In one survey of American millionaires, 62.4 percent said they tracked how much their family spent each year on food, clothing, and shelter. If you're wondering why millionaires need to track their spending, you've got the cause and effect backward: For many, keeping a close eye on expenses was an essential part of stashing away a million dollars.

STEP 1: For the next twenty-four hours, make a note of every penny you spend. You can do it by hand, or on a spreadsheet, or search the app store of your choice for "track spending."

STEP 2: Log on to your bank account and credit card websites to make sure you didn't miss anything, including transactions you may have previously scheduled and forgotten about.

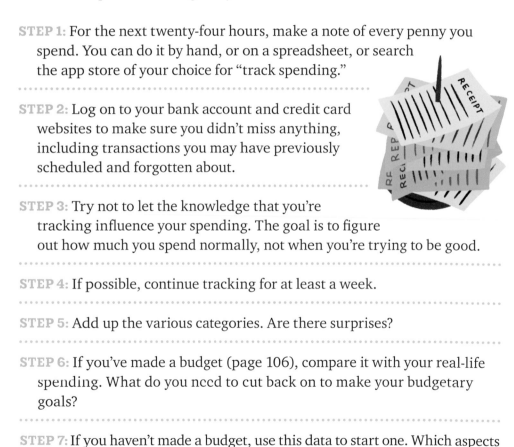

STEP 3: Try not to let the knowledge that you're tracking influence your spending. The goal is to figure out how much you spend normally, not when you're trying to be good.

STEP 4: If possible, continue tracking for at least a week.

STEP 5: Add up the various categories. Are there surprises?

STEP 6: If you've made a budget (page 106), compare it with your real-life spending. What do you need to cut back on to make your budgetary goals?

STEP 7: If you haven't made a budget, use this data to start one. Which aspects of your spending were you happy with? Which would you like to change?

☐ If you've tracked your spending today, count up one additional win.

VALUE EXPERTISE

There's an old story of a factory where a complex piece of machinery breaks down. Nobody can fix it. Finally, they call in a famous engineer who hits it with a hammer. The machine roars back to life.

When the engineer submits a bill for $100,000, the factory owner demands an itemized breakdown. The engineer says, "I billed you $1 for hitting the machine with the hammer. The other $99,999 was for knowing where to hit."

Expertise can't be seen or touched, and it's hard to quantify. That makes it easy to undervalue. But when you buy expertise, you are buying time in its most concentrated form; you're getting the benefits of decades of experience. That's worth paying for.

STEP 1: When deciding whether somebody is worth the price they're charging, factor in expertise. If you spend $100 extra for a plumber with the skill to prevent $500 worth of problems, you've made a great investment.

STEP 2: Also consider expertise when deciding *where* to shop. My neighborhood bookstore charges more than Amazon. But my local bookseller knows every book on her shelves and can recommend them based on my tastes. She's introduced me to some of my favorite authors. That's worth considerably more than a few bucks.

STEP 3: Don't undervalue your own expertise, either. If you've spent years building up a skill, charge appropriately.

☐ If you've taken expertise into account when paying somebody (or when asking to be paid), you're an expert in winning.

SEE THINGS AS MEMORIES

"Buy memories, not things" (page 105) is perfectly good advice—but sometimes you need to buy things. You can't sleep on a fond memory or use it to call your friends.

Once you have a thing, though, hedonic adaptation will set in. You'll find yourself regretting the purchase and being tempted to replace it with something newer and shinier. You can reduce both the regret and the temptation by linking your physical items to more adaptation-resistant memories.

STEP 1: Consider an item you've grown tired of.

STEP 2: Think about the memories you've had with it. Is this an out-of-date cell phone—or the cell phone you used to wish your best friend happy birthday for the past few years?

STEP 3: If you have a specific, practical need to replace the item, that's fair enough. But if you're tempted purely by the lure of the new, ask yourself: Will a replacement come with the same memories?

☐ If you've resisted hedonic adaptation by focusing on happy memories, fondly recall it as a win.

SWITCH

There are many ways companies reward their loyal customers: special perks . . . friendly emails on your birthday . . . and higher prices.

Maybe the last one doesn't feel like much of a reward. But companies routinely reserve their best deals for new customers. In a survey of over sixty-one thousand *Consumer Reports* members, the majority of those who had switched mobile phone providers ended up paying lower monthly bills.

Companies know it's a hassle for you to switch, and they're counting on you to lose money, rather than bother. Prove them wrong.

STEP 1: For recurring expenses like your cell phone plan, check if you're locked in to your current contract. If you are, mark your calendar with the date you'll be free. As soon as you are, see if another provider offers you a better deal.

STEP 2: If switching requires you to call your current provider, tell them the deal their competitor is offering, and see if they'll beat it (or, at least, match it, and save both of you the trouble of switching).

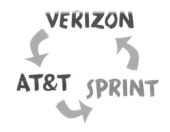

STEP 3: If you can't get a better deal from your current provider, switch to the new one.

STEP 4: Mark your calendar with the date you'll be free to switch from this new contract. As soon as that date arrives, repeat the whole process.

☐ If you've switched providers to get a better deal, switch over to victory.

PAY IN ADVANCE

When does a vacation bring you the most happiness: when you're on a beach in Bermuda, or when you're back home looking through your photos?

The correct answer is, before you even go.

That's right: In a survey of 1,530 people, researchers found that vacations had the greatest happiness-boosting power before they even began. Being on vacation makes you somewhat happier—but looking forward to a vacation makes you happier still.

It may have to do with our old enemy hedonic adaptation. You can get used to being in even the most gorgeous place on earth—but you can't get used to something that hasn't happened yet.

The pleasure of anticipation can be good for your bank account as well. By drawing out your enjoyment of a single purchase, it lets you spend less.

STEP 1: Identify a pleasure you can afford.

STEP 2: Pay for it in advance. Book plane tickets for a trip three months from now. Even better, sign up in advance for a series of small pleasures (page 104), like a bagel-of-the-month club, so you can look forward to it repeatedly. As a bonus, upfront subscriptions can make it easier to surface the cost (next page).

☐ If you've paid in advance for something you're looking forward to, look back on it as a win.

SURFACE THE COST

Lots of us would balk at paying $1,800 a year for a turkey-sandwich subscription but happily hand over $7.50 to a local deli every workday. And yet, mathematically, they're the same. Your bank account doesn't care if the money is taken out a little at a time or all at once. Why should you?

By **surfacing the cost**, you can get a true picture of what seemingly small expenses really cost you.

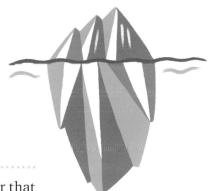

STEP 1: Consider a small amount of money you routinely spend—that bottle of fizzy water you always by with your lunch, for example.

STEP 2: Add up what it costs you over an entire year. $1 on Evian every weekday for 48 weeks adds up to $240.

STEP 3: Ask yourself: Is there a better use for that amount of money? If you're getting lots of small moments of joy (page 104), that's great. But if you'd be just as happy drinking tap water, why not spend that $240 on a nice dinner or two with your best friend?

STEP 4: If you don't want to give up your recurring luxury, you might be able to lower its cost with an upfront investment. If it saves you $1 every work day, a $150 home carbonating kit will pay for itself in six months.

☐ If you've surfaced the full cost for one recurring expense, add it up to one win.

KILL ZOMBIE COSTS

Once upon a time, you visited the gym twice a week. Sadly, that habit has died—but you never canceled your membership, and thus, your subscription costs continue to stagger forward mindlessly. Your gym subscription has become a **zombie cost**. It's time to thwack it on the head with a giant wooden plank.

STEP 1: Look at your credit card statements and bank accounts, line by line. Are there any recurring costs you forgot you signed up for?

STEP 2: If so, cancel them.

STEP 3: While you're at it, surface the cost (page 113) of the subscriptions you *haven't* forgotten.

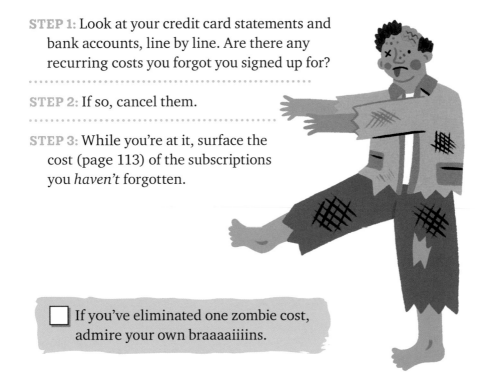

☐ If you've eliminated one zombie cost, admire your own braaaaiiiins.

GIVE THE GIFT OF NOT GIVING GIFTS

You have $10 and I have $10. We can each spend our own money on something we know we'll like. Or we can each guess what the other person will like and buy that. Which one is more likely to result in both of us getting the thing we want? As unsentimental as it might sound, deciding not to exchange gifts with your loved ones might be a wise financial choice that makes everybody happier.

STEP 1: Think of somebody you usually exchange gifts with.

STEP 2: Ask them if exchanging gifts is an important expression of love for them.

STEP 3: If the answer is yes, propose exchanging nonmonetary gifts, like doing errands for each other.

STEP 4: If the answer is no, try skipping the next gift exchange.

STEP 5: If you do want to spend money on each other, see page 116 for tips on how to make the most of it.

☐ If you've agreed not to exchange monetary gifts with somebody, give yourself a win.

GIVE THE GIFT OF TOGETHERNESS

Most economists would agree with my advice to stay away from gift-giving (page 115). But most psychologists wouldn't. In the spirit of fairness, let me present their point of view.

Studies show that money spent on somebody else is more likely to make you happy than money spent on yourself. That includes donations to charity (page 120) as well as gifts to people you know.

When it comes to gift-giving, psychologists have drilled down even further. Based on their research, here's how to give gifts that will make you happier.

STEP 1: Find somebody with whom you have **strong ties**. Psychologists define that as a state of frequent contact and intense feelings.

STEP 2: Give them a gift.

STEP 3: Best of all, give them a gift of an experience that the two of you can share. That will result in a happy memory, which won't lose its luster the way a physical object might (page 105).

STEP 4: Let them reciprocate with a gift of their own. Why rob them of the joy of spending on others?

STEP 5: Studies show that giving a gift to somebody with whom you have **weak ties** is unlikely to make you happier. If you feel obligated to get something for that uncle you only see on Christmas, consider making a donation in his honor to a charity he finds meaningful. It's likely to make you both happier than doling out yet another trinket he'll toss in his closet.

☐ If you've given a shared experience to a close friend, share the win.

BUY TIME

Economist Richard Easterlin discovered what came to be known as the Easterlin Paradox: When countries get wealthier, they don't necessarily get happier. One explanation—advanced by Laura Giurge at the London School of Economics and Politcial Science and Ashley Whillans at Harvard—is that richer countries are more likely to suffer from **time poverty**, the feeling that there aren't enough hours in the day.

If you'd like to feel more time affluent, there are some simple steps you can take.

STEP 1: When you spend discretionary income, buy time instead of stuff. A fancy watch won't give you more free hours in the day. Hiring a neighborhood kid to rake your lawn will.

STEP 2: When you do buy physical objects, prioritize ones that will reduce time spent on unpleasant tasks. Hate housecleaning? A robot vacuum may be a splurge you won't regret.

STEP 3: Paradoxically, studies show that taking time to do good deeds makes you feel *more* time rich. Volunteer at a charity, help a friend, or just linger for a split second and hold the door for the next person.

STEP 4: Meditation has also been linked to increased feelings of time affluence. We all have the same twenty-four hours a day, but meditators may get more joy out of each one.

☐ If you've increased your feeling of time affluence, you've got time to appreciate your win.

LOCK UP TIME THIEVES

From checking your credit report (page 89) to avoiding scams (page 132), you take multiple steps to prevent people from stealing your money. And you know that time is money. So what steps do you take to stop people from stealing your time?

While money thieves are frequently individuals, time thieves tend to be well-funded corporations. Every time you use social media, you're adding value to some Silicon Valley corporation. If you find meaningful connections on Facebook, then it's a fair exchange. But if not, then you've had hours of your life stolen for somebody else's benefit.

STEP 1: If your operating system lets you track how many hours you spend on certain websites or apps, keep an eye on how many hours of free labor you give social media corporations.

STEP 2: Identify other areas where you regret time spent. Do you watch more TV than you'd like? (Remember: The goal isn't to feel bad about frivolous things that bring you joy; it's to stop wasting time on things that don't.)

STEP 3: Put small obstacles in your way. Leave your remote control in a different room than the TV. Delete social media apps from your phone. You don't have to make things impossible; often, just creating an extra step in the process is enough to stop you from completing it mindlessly.

STEP 4: If you're still spending time in ways you regret, see my tips on breaking bad habits (page 44).

> ☐ If you've liberated even a single minute from the time thieves, you've stolen victory from the jaws of defeat.

HELP LOST ELECTRONICS COME HOME

Nowadays, many of us leave the house carrying more computing power than any given Apollo rocket. And while our gizmos may not cost quite the $25 billion that the moon landing did, they are among the most expensive items we take to strange places.

And the personal information tucked away on them is even more valuable. Take a few minutes to make lost gadgets harder to crack, but easier to return.

STEP 1: Collect the valuable electronics you routinely take out of the house.

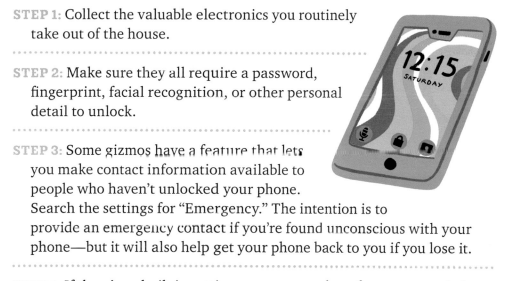

STEP 2: Make sure they all require a password, fingerprint, facial recognition, or other personal detail to unlock.

STEP 3: Some gizmos have a feature that lets you make contact information available to people who haven't unlocked your phone. Search the settings for "Emergency." The intention is to provide an emergency contact if you're found unconscious with your phone—but it will also help get your phone back to you if you lose it.

STEP 4: If there's no built-in setting, use a screenshot of your contact info as your lock screen. *Do* include something other than your mobile phone number, or the person who finds it will end up calling the phone itself. *Don't* include any information that might hint at your passwords.

STEP 5: If your device has a tracking feature, make sure you can access it from a different device.

☐ If a stranger can get an alternate contact number from your electronic devices, but no other information, download a win.

GIVE AWAY YOUR HARD-EARNED CASH

You wouldn't expect a book on being richer to advise giving away your money. "If I wanted to have *less* money," you might be saying, "I'd have bought *Live Poorer Now*."

I can't argue with the math: Giving away money means less money.

But a nationwide survey by researchers at the Harvard Business School and the University of British Columbia found that the amount of money people spent on themselves had nothing to do with how happy they were. The happiest people were the ones who spent the most on *others*.

In other words, giving your money away can make you happier . . . and isn't that why you wanted the money in the first place?

STEP 1: Identify an amount of money you were planning to spend on an unneeded purchase for yourself.

STEP 2: Give it to a charity you find meaningful. For an extra happiness boost, divide it into twelve installments and set up an automatic monthly donation, allowing you to break one purchase into multiple smaller ones (page 104).

☐ If you've given money to a worthwhile cause, give a win to yourself.

REVIEW THE REVIEWERS

Fake reviews are a big business. According to consumer magazine *Which?*, online fake-review rings can have up to two hundred thousand members. They get free items from unscrupulous manufacturers in exchange for five-star raves.

No matter how much AuthenticAmericanDad23458 enthuses about those headphones, do a little digging before you buy.

STEP 1: Amazon and many other websites let you see reviews with a specific star rating. Make a point of looking at reviews with four, three, or two stars; often, those will be more nuanced and realistic than reviews at the extremes.

STEP 2: If you are going to buy a product based on one particularly enthusiastic review, click on the reviewer's name to see what else they've written. If they've churned out nothing but five-star raves, take their enthusiasm with a grain of salt.

STEP 3: Be especially careful when it comes to food, medical, or electrical products. A bad pair of mittens can annoy you. A bad desk lamp can burn your house down.

STEP 4: When in doubt, buy from an independent brick-and-mortar store with salespeople who know their subject. They may have an incentive to sell you stuff—but they don't have an incentive to set you on fire.

☐ If you've exercised caution in dealing with online reviews, rate yourself five stars.

GO GREEN (AS IN MONEY)

The right thing isn't always the most profitable thing. One happy exception: Cutting back on waste is good for the environment *and* your wallet.

STEP 1: Stop spending money on disposable items. Instead of cycling through expensive plastic razor heads, get a razor that lets you use double-sided safety blades. They cost pennies per use and send zero plastic to landfills.

STEP 2: Insulate your home to save money on heating bills (and prevent waste heat). While you're at it, turn down your thermostat a degree or two in winter and wear an extra layer. If you find yourself blasting the AC so high in summer you have to wear a sweater, turning the thermostat up is a money-saving tip you can feel good about.

STEP 3: Check for leaks and drips in your home water system.

STEP 4: Speaking of water, carry a reusable bottle with you and fill it for free at taps and drinking fountains. Never again throw money away on something that literally falls from the sky.

STEP 5: Wash your clothes in cold water to save electricity costs.

STEP 6: If you're just cooking for one or two, consider getting a countertop air fryer, pressure cooker, or slow cooker. They often use less energy than a full-size appliance and can end up paying for themselves within a year.

STEP 7: If you find yourself needing to run the dishwasher before it's full, buy more of whatever you're short of—plates, silverware, or glasses. Fewer dishwasher cycles means less wasted water and energy.

☐ If you've done one thing to help the environment *and* your budget, harvest a green win.

MAKE A BUY-ON-SALE LIST

Ah, sales. In theory, a delightful opportunity to save money. In practice, a tempting opportunity to waste it.

By deciding what to buy before the sale begins, you can resist getting swept up in the thrill of the hunt.

STEP 1: Start a buy-on-sale list. Keep it someplace you'll be able to access easily when a thought occurs to you—whether that's a file on your phone or a piece of paper on your fridge.

STEP 2: When you're tempted to buy anything, ask yourself if you can wait until it goes on sale. If the answer is yes, add it to your list.

STEP 3: When stores drop their prices for Black Friday, or Presidents' Day, or International Day Made Up to Sell Stuff, look for the items on your list.

STEP 4: Before buying, check the item's price history (next page) to make sure you really are getting a good deal.

STEP 5: If you're tempted to buy something not on your list, ask yourself: If I didn't realize I needed it before it went on sale, do I really need it? If you have any doubt, wait until the sale is over and put it on your buy-on-sale list for next time. If you still want it, then go ahead and get it.

SALE
*STUFF YOU ACTUALLY WANT TO BUY

☐ If you've made a buy-on-sale list (or used the list during a sale), buy yourself a bargain-price trophy.

COMPARE PRICES WITH THE PAST

Today, a copy of *Action Comics* #1, featuring the very first appearance of Superman, is worth more than $3 million. If you had a time machine, you could go back to June 1938 and buy a copy for the cover price of 10 cents.

Alas, I haven't unlocked the secrets of literal time travel. But by using a price-comparison website, you can wait until a product's current price dips back to its historical low. It's like traveling back in time to a sale price you missed. Now *that's* a superpower.

STEP 1: Think about a product you'd like to buy that you don't need urgently. See how much it currently costs at a retailer you trust.

STEP 2: Go to a website that offers price histories. As I write this, **CamelCamelCamel.com** is great for seeing what things have cost on Amazon, and **JoinHoney.com** is excellent for other retailers.

STEP 3: See if your product has been cheaper in the recent past.

STEP 4: If it's been cheaper in the past, ask the website to alert you by email when the price drops back down.

STEP 5: If it's as cheap as it's ever been, go ahead and buy it (but do a Next Tuesday test first (page 99).

☐ If you've checked past prices before buying, give yourself a present-day win.

MEAL PLAN/MEAL PREP

It's 7:30 on a weekday evening. You're starving and there's nothing in the fridge, so you order takeout. You end up spending three times what it would have cost to make something yourself, and by the time you get home to eat it, the food is cold.

With a little planning, you could be chowing down on a cheaper and healthier meal, hot out of the oven.

STEP 1: Plan out your meals for the week. If it fits your budget, there's no shame in including a certain number of takeout or store-bought-ready meals in your plan.

STEP 2: Think about how the leftovers from one meal can flow frugally into the next. Make roast chicken on Monday. Use the leftover meat for Taco Tuesday. Use the bones for soup on Wednesday.

STEP 3: Look for opportunities to prepare food in advance, saving you time at the end of a long day. Can you freeze something on Sunday, then leave it to defrost in the fridge while you're at work on Thursday? Or premix a big container of dry rub that you can use on future barbecues?

STEP 4: Oncc you've got your meal plan, work out a shopping plan. If you can buy for an entire week's worth of meals at once, you'll save on transportation costs, too.

☐ If you've planned or prepared one meal in advance, take a win right now.

Weekly Food Planner

MONDAY

TUESDAY

WEDNESDAY

THURSDAY

FRIDAY

SATURDAY

SUNDAY

THINK LIKE SAM VIMES

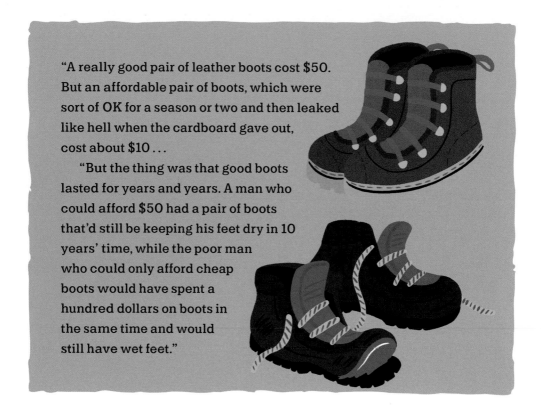

"A really good pair of leather boots cost $50. But an affordable pair of boots, which were sort of OK for a season or two and then leaked like hell when the cardboard gave out, cost about $10 . . .

"But the thing was that good boots lasted for years and years. A man who could afford $50 had a pair of boots that'd still be keeping his feet dry in 10 years' time, while the poor man who could only afford cheap boots would have spent a hundred dollars on boots in the same time and would still have wet feet."

So opines the fictional Samuel Vimes in Terry Pratchett's novel *Men at Arms*. Pratchett wasn't the first to notice the phenomenon, but he articulated it so vividly that it's become known as the Vimes Theory of Socioeconomic Unfairness.

In this entry, I talk about staying on the right side of Vimes's equation. Consider using some of the money you save to help those who are trapped on the wrong side (page 120).

STEP 1: Don't compare items based on sticker price. Instead, figure out how much they'll cost per year. In the long run, a $50 coat that will fall apart by April is more expensive than a $400 coat you'll wear for a decade.

STEP 2: Make sure you factor in consumables. If you're buying a car, work out how much each model will likely cost you in gas. If you're refrigerator shopping, think about lifetime electricity costs.

STEP 3: Also factor in the ability to repair or upgrade. As Vimes knew, resoleable shoes can live multiple lifetimes.

STEP 4: Don't let the Vimes principle trick you into spending beyond your means. If you're tempted to buy a long-lasting item on credit, make sure to consider the ultimate value and cost (page 84).

☐ If you've factored in lifetime running costs before making a purchase, give yourself a lifetime win.

STOP WASTING FOOD

Americans waste $216 billion worth of food every year, with an average family of four throwing out $1,600 in produce alone. A meal plan (page 126) will help you avoid buying more food than you need. Once it's in your home, you can take a few simple steps to make sure you use it before it goes bad.

STEP 1: Put a good quality permanent pen (I use a Sharpie) in your kitchen. When you open food, write today's date on the package. You'll never again have to throw out a half-full bottle of ketchup because you can't remember how long ago you opened it.

STEP 2: Keep a roll of masking tape next to your Sharpie. Use it to put the date on reusable containers.

STEP 3: When food passes a "use by" date, it's no longer safe to eat; throw it out. But food past a "best by" date isn't necessarily dangerous; it just might not taste as fresh. Use it up as soon as possible, but don't feel obligated to trash it immediately.

☐ If you've taken one step to prevent food waste, feast on a win.

USE A PASSWORD MANAGER

Using the same password for every website is a major security problem. If one site gets hacked, thieves can access every single account you have.

But using a new password for every site is a major *memory* problem. Was your banking password l3F@jr1WFF07 or was that for eBay?

Fortunately, there's a solution to both problems: a password manager. A good password manager stores all your passwords in a secure, encrypted file. All you have to remember is the one password that unlocks the password manager. Sometimes you don't even need to remember that; you can often unlock a manager with your thumbprint or your face.

And the best password managers will sync across devices, so if you create a login on your computer, it'll be there waiting on your phone.

STEP 1: If you're staying with the same electronics ecosystem, see if there's a built-in password manager. On Android/Chrome, it's Google Password Manager. On iPhone/Mac, it's iCloud Keychain. Often, you can find them by going to the settings and searching for "passwords."

STEP 2: If not (or if you don't like the built-in option), it's well worth paying for a replacement that works for you. If it saves you from a single security breach, you'll have gotten your money's worth. The best option changes from year to year. As I write this, Dashlane and 1Password are frequently well-reviewed.

STEP 3: Now that you don't have to remember your passwords, use a different long and complex password for every site you visit.

☐ If you've used a password manager, the secret word is WINNER.

BE SCAM SMART

You work hard for your money. Don't let scammers steal it from you.

STEP 1: Caller ID can be easily spoofed. Use the same caution and common sense whether or not a call appears to come from a legitimate company.

STEP 2: Never give out your credit card, Social Security number, or other personal information to somebody who calls you.

STEP 3: If somebody calls you claiming to be from your bank or credit card company, tell them you'll call back. Hang up and dial the phone number on your card.

STEP 4: If a caller claims to be from a computer or internet company and tells you to type in a web address or install any app or extension, don't do it. Hang up. If you have a tech support question, dial the number shown on your bill.

STEP 5: If an error or pop-up message appears on your screen telling you to call a phone number, don't call. That's not how legitimate error messages work.

STEP 6: Scammers may try to make you panic to stop you from noticing holes in their story. If somebody claims you're about to be arrested, or your property is on the verge of being seized, ask them to send you a written notice. Then hang up. If you're worried, find a legitimate number for whatever organization they claimed to be from and call to check their story.

STEP 7: If you get an email from somebody who claims to be spying on you and offers you one of your passwords for proof, don't worry. They haven't actually been spying on you; they got a list of thousands of passwords from a website leak, and they've set up a script to mail each one. Change that password as soon as possible, but otherwise ignore the threat.

STEP 8: If you do fall victim to a scammer, don't beat yourself up. It can happen to anybody. Call your credit card company or bank as soon as possible to alert them and to contest the charges. Replace any affected cards as soon as possible. And be alert for follow-up scams, where crooks call pretending to be from law enforcement or some other agency that can recover your money, if you'll just give them all your credit card info first . . .

☐ If you've dodged one scam, give yourself a victory that nobody can steal.

ONE LAST TIP: LIVE LIKE A MILLIONAIRE

Thomas Stanley and William Danko spent twenty years studying America's millionaires. Some of their subjects had huge salaries or vast inherited wealth. But a surprising number started without an inheritance and earned their high net worth through not-especially-lucrative jobs like paving contractor or rice farmer.

How did these "working-class millionaires" do it? In large part, by living lifestyles that were as unmillionairelike as possible. It turns out that involves many of the techniques in this book.

> To learn more, read *The Millionaire Next Door* by Thomas J. Stanley and William D. Danko.

STEP 1: Force yourself into frugality. Stanley and Danko's millionaires didn't just live within their means; they created "an artificial economic environment of scarcity" by socking their money in investment accounts before they had the chance to spend it. In other words, they paid themselves first (page 65), investing an average 20 percent of their annual income.

STEP 2: Work toward owning your own home (page 68), and then stay in that home as long as possible.

STEP 3: You don't have to buy the cheapest option for everything... but buy the cheapest thing you can get that will last. See page 128 for tips.

STEP 4: Have concrete financial goals (page 5) and a plan for achieving them (page 6).

YOUR LOCAL MILLIONAIRE

☐ If you've done something to live like one of Stanley and Danko's frugal millionaires, give yourself a million wins.

Acknowledgments

In 2019, my fantastic agent, Ammi-Joan Paquette, recognized that I'd click with the brilliant and passionate staff of Odd Dot and suggested I stop by their offices and meet them. This is the fifth book to come out of that meeting. My 101st tip on how to be richer is "Have Joan Paquette as your agent."

Speaking of Odd Dot's brilliant and passionate staff, thank you to Nathalie Le Du, Christina Quintero, Kate Avino, Jen Healey, Barbara Cho, Kathy Wielgosz, Tracy Koontz, Caitlyn Hunter, and Caitlyn Ward. I'm especially grateful to my editor Justin Krasner for trusting me with a fourth book in the Be Better Now series.

Thank you to Rachel Sanborn Lawrence, a certified financial planner and the founder of Plan Ventures Consulting and Reverie Wealth. She read the manuscript, told me what I got wrong, and suggested numerous helpful additions. It's through her, for example, that I learned about one-number budgeting. If any errors remain despite her expert feedback, the fault is entirely mine.

And above all, thank you Lauren, Erin, and Joe, for your patience over the many days I hid away in my office to write this book, and for your love and support always. You make me feel truly rich.